Taking the
CUNY Assessment
Test in Writing

Taking the CUNY Assessment Test in Writing

Laurence Berkley
Borough of Manhattan Community College

Bedford/St. Martin's   Boston ◆ New York

Manufactured in the United States of America.

6 5 4 3 2 1
f e d c b a

For information, write: Bedford/St. Martin's, 75 Arlington Street,
Boston, MA 02116   (617-399-4000)

ISBN: 978-1-4576-0228-3

Contents

Chapter 7: Additional Practice for the CATW 49

Chapter 8: Correcting Common Errors 57

Some Commonly Confused Words 63

Some Commonly Misspelled Words 65

Answers to Some of the Exercises in Chapter 5 67

Preface for Instructors

This CUNY Assessment Test in Writing (CATW) preparation guide provides an overview of the format of the CATW, explains the rhetorical structure of the typical reading passage found on the exam, and maps out the directions that students are expected to follow as they craft their written responses from the passage. It contains the following:

- An explanation of the scoring rubric, including an explanation of what the scores on the CATW indicate

- Sample responses to these passages, and explanations of the scores they would likely receive

- Strategies that will help students to produce upper-level responses to the reading passages

- A set of reading passages that can be used as writing prompts for practice tests

- A review of key issues in grammar and punctuation for native and non-native speakers

In other words, this guide provides all the information students need to prepare for the CATW.

Used in a developmental writing course, this guide will give instructors the teaching strategies and models they need to help their students write upper-range responses to the CATW passage. The strongest written responses to the CATW passage are those that demonstrate more than just an adequate understanding of the passage. This guide challenges students to identify the complexities that any reading passage attempts to communicate and to respond to those complexities in ways that are thoughtful, insightful, and articulate.

The guide can, of course, function as a workbook for students preparing on their own for the CATW placement exam or exit exam. With this workbook, students can familiarize themselves in advance with the quality of work they will need to produce on the exam in order to bypass placement in a developmental writing course and qualify for a college-level English composition course. In addition, students who are already enrolled in an ESL or developmental writing course can use this guide on their own to supplement their out-of-class work.

Instructors of freshman composition will also find that the sections in the guide on summary, organization, and essay development provide valuable introductory and review material for the rigors of a freshman writing course, since the format of the CATW is not unlike the format of the final exam used in many freshman English composition courses. While the reading passages of the CATW are shorter and more accessible than the passages generally used in freshman-level writing courses, instructors of freshman English may consider using this preparation guide in the earlier stages of their composition courses, until they move to longer readings with more complex argumentative structures.

Acknowledgments

This book could not have been written without a combination of fortuitous influences. First of all, I thank my colleagues at BMCC who participated in my CATW workshops during the fall semester of 2010, for trusting my interpretations of the new CATW exam but also balancing those interpretations by offering valuable and compelling suggestions when my interpretations appeared too inflexible. The task force at CUNY Assessment that brought forward the CATW — Eve Zarin, Gay Brooks, Frederick DeNaples, and Sue Young — provided the foundation for my understanding of the CATW rubric and the knowledge of how to go about teaching my students to prepare for the exam. I thank the certified CATW scorers who have worked with me as BMCC's Chief Reader and who are, without fear of misstatement, the most compassionate people I have ever worked with. I thank, too, Professor Doris Barkin for piloting the passages that are included in this book and offering suggestions that only improved them. I particularly thank the Chair of the English Department at BMCC, Dr. Joyce Harte, who honored me with her endorsement by recommending me to Brian Donnellan, BMCC's representative at Bedford/ St. Martin's. The final decisions of Alexis Walker and Jane Carter, the patient editors on this project, were invaluable and correct and always in the best interest of the project.

Many faculty members reviewed the manuscript and offered suggestions that greatly improved the book: Steve Belluscio, Borough of Manhattan Community College; Beth Counihan, Queensborough Community College; Cheryl Fish, Borough of Manhattan Community College; Barbara Guinan, New York City College of Technology; Ronna Levy, Kingsborough Community College; David Rothman, Queensborough Community College; Enid Stubin, Kingsborough Community College; Claudia Zuluaga, John Jay College of Criminal Justice.

I would finally like to thank Gabrielle Bernard for being there always, for providing advice when asked, and for withholding advice when unasked.

Taking the CUNY Assessment Test in Writing

1 Introducing the CATW

The CUNY Assessment Test in Writing (CATW) is a standardized writing exam offered by four-year colleges and community colleges in the City University of New York (CUNY) system. You do *not* have to take the CATW if you already have a Bachelor's Degree from an accredited college or university in the United States *or* if you received a score of 480 or better on the SAT I Verbal or the SAT Critical Reading exam,[1] an ACT English score of 20 or better, or a New York State Regents score in English of 75 or above. The CATW is also administered as an exit exam to students enrolled in upper-level ESL or English developmental writing courses to determine their readiness for college-level freshman composition courses.

The Format of the Exam

There are two parts to the CATW. The first part consists of a reading passage of approximately 300–350 words, edited to reflect an eleventh- or twelfth-grade reading level. The second part consists of writing directions that guide you in your response to the passage. These directions ask you to demonstrate understanding of the passage and to organize a critical response using summary, analysis, and supporting evidence.

THE READING PASSAGE

Reading passages used for the CATW commonly fall into two categories: one presents a provocative viewpoint on a familiar topic; the other presents opposing viewpoints in the form of a debate. The first type of passage might argue, for example, that video games provide teenagers with learning and motor skills that are important in life. This position is provocative because it contradicts the conventional wisdom that excessive exposure to video games is, at best, a waste of time and, at worst, an activity that leads to social isolation and intellectual backwardness. Your response should indicate that you understand that this argument offers an alternative to the usual point of view, and it should demonstrate your understanding of the argument's complexities. You will score higher in the domains that assess Critical Response and Development of Ideas if you are able to demonstrate your understanding of the fact that your arguments are responding to arguments in the passage.

The other type of passage that is commonly used on the CATW presents a debate between opposing positions. For example, one position might hold that exercise is a good thing, that it promotes good health and mental stability, relieves stress, and combats obesity. The second position might claim that exercising inevitably leads to injuries and that the effect of such injuries outweighs other health benefits. In this type of passage, the debate is always left unresolved. That is, the reader is left to decide which position is most convincing. Your written response to this kind of passage may either argue for one of the two positions or compare these two perspectives as an ongoing debate.

---

[1] Before March 2005, the Critical Reading section of the SAT was called the SAT I Verbal section.

Scoring the Exam

The exam is scored by two independent and certified CATW readers according to the scoring criteria, or **rubric**, outlined below. The CATW measures the student's writing skills in the following five areas, or **domains:**

1. Critical response to task and text
2. Development of the writer's ideas
3. Structure of the response
4. Language use: Sentence structure and word choice
5. Language use: Grammar, usage, and mechanics

THE FIVE DOMAINS IN DETAIL

The five domains, or areas of assessment, by which the CATW response is scored are described in greater detail below.

Critical Response to Task and Text

To assess the critical response to the writing task and text, graders evaluate the following:

- The completeness with which you respond to the writing task as outlined in the writing directions
- Your understanding of the passage and your ability to demonstrate that understanding through your summary and your analysis of the passage

It might help to think of your written response as your "conversation" or "dialogue" with the passage, and this domain as an assessment of the thoughtfulness or insightfulness of that "conversation" or "dialogue." Graders are interested in how fully you respond to the passage, how insightful your understanding of the main arguments or ideas in the passage is, how well you integrate ideas from the passage into your summary, and how critically you analyze and support those ideas.

Development of the Writer's Ideas

When graders evaluate the development of the writer's ideas, they consider the following:

- The effectiveness with which you develop your own ideas in response to ideas that are introduced in the passage, using appropriate techniques such as summary and evaluation
- The skill with which you use details and evidence from the passage in combination with the evidence from your reading, your schoolwork, and your own experience to support your ideas

Here again, graders are interested in how you respond to details in the passage: How effectively do you support your ideas with relevant details from the passage and from your own experiences?

Structure of the Response

When graders evaluate the structure of the response, they consider the following:

- The presentation of ideas in support of a central focus
- The logical progression of ideas in the response
- The effectiveness of the transitions between ideas

Graders are concerned with your ability to write a coherent, well-organized response. A coherent written response will have a central focus and a clear beginning, middle, and end, and it will move logically and smoothly from one idea to the next as it advances through the writing tasks.

Language Use: Sentence Structure and Word Choice

When graders evaluate your sentence structure and word choice, they consider the following:

- The grammatical correctness of sentence structures
- The variety of sentence structures and how they present relationships among ideas
- The variety and accuracy of vocabulary

Graders are concerned with your ability to demonstrate command of sentence structure and word choice. They want to see that you show control of your sentence structures and that your sentences clarify the ideas you are conveying. They want you to use words that clearly convey meaning, to use a range of vocabulary words (not just repeat the same words), and to use language in a way that demonstrates an ability to suggest a range of meanings.

Language Use: Grammar, Usage, and Mechanics

When graders evaluate your grammar, usage, and mechanics, they consider the following:

- The use of standard American English grammar
- The use of punctuation and mechanics according to the rules of standard American English
- Appropriate usage of words and phrases

Graders will look to see that your written response follows the conventions of standard American English composition. They want to see that your writing follows the rules that govern the construction of sentences, phrases, and words (i.e., grammar). They want to see that your response conforms to correct written and idiomatic form (i.e., usage). They want you to demonstrate that you understand the guidelines that control the presentation of the written response, such as spelling, punctuation, capitalization, indentation, and quotation.

SCORE POINTS

On the next page is a grid explaining what each score point means in the different domains, or categories, of grading. Read it to get a sense of what scorers are looking for at each level. This grid is a simpler version of the official grid that the CUNY Office of Assessment offers students in their CATW Student Handbook (www.cuny.edu/academics/testing/cuny-assessment-tests /resources/StudentHandbookCATWWeb.pdf) As you move vertically through the score points from 6 to 1, notice the words and phrases that qualify the scores within each domain. This simplified scoring scale may help you to understand the scoring process more easily.

	Critical Response to Task & Text	Essay Development	Essay Structure	Sentence Variety/ Word Choice	Grammar, Usage, Mechanics
6	Thoughtful and insightful integration of ideas; thorough understanding	Fully developed; skillful and effective support of ideas	Well-designed progression of ideas; sophisticated and effective transitions	Well-controlled sentences, effective variety; sophisticated word choice	Strong command; meaning clear throughout
5	Effective integration of ideas; good understanding	Well developed; usually skillful and effective support of ideas	Clear plan, some progression of ideas; clear transitions	Sentences usually well controlled, effective variety; usually specific word choice	Good command; meaning is usually clear
4	Competent integration of ideas; consistent understanding	Competent development; details from text and experience competently support ideas	Evident plan, competent support of central focus; simple and obvious transitions	Competent sentence control, some variety; general but clear word choice	Competent command; meaning is mostly correct, usually clear
3	Uneven integration of some ideas; superficial and incomplete understanding	General and uneven development; some support of ideas	Basic or uneven; sometimes supports central focus; simple and obvious transitions	Uneven control, a little variety; simple but usually clear word choice	Uneven command; meaning is usually correct, some distracting errors
2	Little integration of ideas; weak understanding	Weak development; brief, general, or inadequate support of ideas	Unclear connections between ideas; few transitions	Weak control, little, if any, variety; simple, often unclear word choice	Weak command; meaning sometimes correct but often distracting
1	Minimal, if any, integration of ideas; little, if any, understanding	Minimal or no development; brief, general, or unclear support of ideas	Unclear or nonexistent central focus; few, if any, transitions	Minimal or no control; unclear word choice	Minimal command; meaning is unclear

Chapter 6 includes sample essays demonstrating what responses at each level might look like.

HOW THE CATW IS SCORED

This section explains how the CATW is scored. Your exam will be graded by two scorers. Your scores in the first three domains—those that consider your critical response, your ability to develop your ideas, and your ability to structure the response—will be multiplied by two and then added to your scores on the two language domains. Ultimately, your final score will fall somewhere between 16 and 96. For instance, consider the following example:

The first scorer rates the exam a 4 on each of the first three domains and a 3 on the two language domains. The second scorer gives the first three domains two 4s and a 3, and gives the exam a 3 on the two language domains.

When you add the scores on the first three domains you get 4 + 4 + 4 + 4 + 4 + 3 = 23. Multiply that number by 2 and the result is 46. Then add the language scores together: 3 + 3 + 3 + 3 = 12. Finally, add 46 + 12 for a total of 58 points.

Here's another way to look at it:

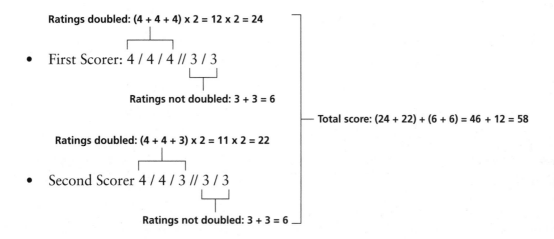

To place into freshman composition, you need a score of 56 or higher.

Rater Score	Score Interpretation	Weighted Total	
6	Superior performance with insight, creativeness	88–96	
5	Effective performance with mastery and control	72–87	
4	Consistent demonstration of competence, errors do not interfere with coherence	56–71	Passing = 56 and above
3	Uneven performance, a basic ability, but significant errors are apparent	40–55	
2	Weak attempt, lapses into incoherence	24–39	
1	Little or no competency	16–23	

2   The Writing Directions

The CATW consists of a passage of 300–350 words followed by writing directions that guide you in your response to the passage. Although the CATW uses many different passages on a variety of topics, the directions always stay the same. Familiarizing yourself with these directions before you take the exam will help you respond more effectively than you would were you to read and analyze them for the first time on exam day.

Here are the directions:

> Read the passage above and write an essay responding to the ideas it presents. In your essay, be sure to summarize the passage in your own words, stating the author's most important ideas. Develop your essay by identifying one idea in the passage that you feel is especially significant, and explain its significance. Support your claims with evidence or examples drawn from what you have read, learned in school, and/or personally experienced.
>
> Remember to review your essay and make any changes or corrections that are needed to help your reader follow your thinking. You will have 90 minutes to complete your essay.

Summarize: State the author's most important ideas in your own words.

Develop: Identify a significant idea, and explain why it is important or significant.

Support: Use details from your experiences in school, your reading, or your life to make your claims believable.

The three writing tasks highlighted above—summarize, develop, and support—are central to your success on the exam.

There is other important information in the directions as well: You are encouraged to read the passage (you should probably read it at least twice) and respond to the ideas it presents. This means you must make sure your response sticks to the author's ideas.

You are also reminded to review your written response and make changes or corrections. In other words, edit and proofread your work to make sure that your focus is clear and that your supporting evidence is relevant. Also, correct any errors in grammar, spelling, and punctuation.

Finally, the directions indicate that you will have ninety minutes (an hour and a half) to craft your response. Be sure you pace yourself: You will need to spend the first block of time (fifteen minutes) reading the passage through *twice* (!) and underlining the author's central ideas. Spend the next few minutes (five) organizing those main ideas so that they can be used in the writing of your summary. Spend most of the time (forty-five minutes to an hour) drafting your response, but save a few minutes at the end (five or ten) to edit and proofread your response. You are allowed to use a paper dictionary, so use the time you have at the end to check the spelling of words that you are unsure of.

3 Writing a Response to a Sample CATW Passage

Let's consider a sample CATW passage, the kind of passage you might expect to find on the CATW or in a course designed to prepare you for the CATW as an exit exam.

Read the passage and the directions that follow.

The Lottery Is for Losers
by Mary Pickford

America was born and raised on the lottery. In 1612, the English government held a lottery to finance the first European settlement in the New World in Jamestown, Virginia. During the 18th and 19th centuries, as America grew from a colony into a republic, lotteries financed its wars, its places of worship and education, and a host of other public projects. Eventually, however, the lottery became associated with gambling, and in 1892 the Supreme Court banned lotteries altogether. In 1964, states revived the lottery as a way of generating revenue without raising taxes. Apparently, gambling was not so objectionable as long as it produced social benefits.

The biggest problem with the lottery is that it makes no economic sense to play it. The odds of winning are 1 in 14–175 million, depending on the game. And yet, millions of people spend billions of dollars a year hoping to beat these odds. Seductive advertisements tell us that "you've got to be in it to win it," but what they do not tell us is that no one ever wins the lottery because it's just not designed for winning.

The lottery does, however, begin to make sense once we recognize its value as entertainment. Who can deny the thrill that accompanies the purchase of the magic tickets, or the drama as the numbers roll down the chute? Even the disappointment of losing somehow teases us by reminding us of the power of our desires. The lottery represents the American dream of limitless wealth with no effort and little investment. It makes the dream possible even as it makes the reality impossible. Let's not forget that the function of the lottery is, and always has been, the financing of the operations of local and state government, not the fulfillment of the dreams of those who are addicted to it.

Once upon a time, the cigarette and liquor industries were required to disclose the dangers of their products. It's about time that the government agencies that run the lottery were held accountable for the realities of their product. They need to make certain things clear: Who really benefits from the lottery? Where does all the money really go? And why doesn't anyone ever win?

WRITING DIRECTIONS

Read the passage above and write an essay responding to the ideas it presents. In your essay, be sure to summarize the passage in your own words, stating the author's most important ideas. Develop your essay by identifying one idea in the passage that you feel is especially significant, and explain its significance. Support your claims with evidence or examples drawn from what you have read, learned in school, and/or personally experienced.

Remember to review your essay and make any changes or corrections that are needed to help your reader follow your thinking. You will have 90 minutes to complete your essay.

Read the passage the first time to get the general sense of what it is saying. As you read, try to answer the following questions: What is the passage about? What are its central ideas and its key supporting points? What conclusion, if any, does the author arrive at? Write down the key words and phrases that come to mind as you answer these questions. These words and phrases should eventually find their way into your written response, but you will need to write them down first because otherwise you will forget them.

As you read the passage a second time, underline or make a check beside the author's main ideas, the ones that appear most important in the passage. Try to separate the main ideas from the specific evidence (such as dates, numbers, statistics, examples) the author uses to support them. For your summary, you are only concerned with the author's main ideas.

After reading through the passage a second time and underlining the author's main ideas, your passage might look something like this:

America was born and raised on the lottery. In 1612, the English government held a lottery to finance the first European settlement in the New World in Jamestown, Virginia. During the 18th and 19th centuries, as America grew from a colony into a republic, lotteries financed its wars, its places of worship and education, and a host of other public projects. Eventually, however, the lottery became associated with gambling, and in 1892 the Supreme Court banned lotteries altogether. In 1964, states revived the lottery as away of generating revenue without raising taxes. Apparently, gambling was not so objectionable as long as it produced social benefits.

The biggest problem with the lottery is that it makes no economic sense to play it. The odds of winning are 1 in 14–175 million, depending on the game. And yet, millions of people spend billions of dollars a year hoping to beat these odds. Seductive advertisements tell us that "you've got to be in it to win," but what they do not tell us is that no one ever wins the lottery because it's just not designed for winning.

The lottery does, however, begin to make sense once we recognize its value as entertainment. Who can deny the thrill that accompanies the purchase of the magic tickets, or the drama as the numbers roll down the chute? Even the disappointment of losing somehow teases us by reminding us of the power of our desires. The lottery represents the American dream of limitless wealth with no effort and little investment. It makes the dream possible even as it makes the reality impossible. Let's not forget that the function of the lottery is, and always has been, the financing of the operations of local and state government, not the fulfillment of the dreams of those who are addicted to it.

Once upon a time, the cigarette and liquor industries were required to disclose the dangers of their products. It's about time that the government agencies that run the lottery were held accountable for the realities of their product. They need to make certain things clear: Who really benefits from the lottery? Where does all the money really go? And why doesn't anyone ever win?

Often, the central idea will be stated in the first or last paragraph (or both). The middle paragraphs are likely to provide examples and can be summed up briefly.

Now Try It Yourself!

Read the entire passage below once to get the general idea of its meaning, and then a second time to identify the author's main ideas. Underline those words and phrases that convey the author's main ideas.

Go to College
by Arthur Digby Sellers

Every parent of every confused 17 year old has heard the same arguments: Why should I bother going to college? What am I going to learn in college that I can't learn in the real world? Their arguments usually follow the same path:

- Some of America's most famous billionaires did not go to college so why should I?

- I can learn so much more by traveling around the world for four years so why don't you just give me the money you would have spent on my education and let me travel?

- I can begin working immediately and make more money right away than if I wait four years.

To this imaginary Bill Gates, or Magellan, I recommend to the parent five good answers. I used them with my children and they worked. They went to college and I convinced them with these arguments:

(1) You will be exposed to a body of knowledge in the form of books and lectures that you should know if you are to be regarded as educated. It may not seem important to you now that you know how the structure of the universe has changed in the last 1500 years, or the details of America's racial history, or that Gregor Samsa awoke one morning to find that he had been transformed into a monstrous vermin, but these things are important. It grants you membership to a special club to which it is better to belong than not belong.

(2) You have the opportunity to postpone for four years an important life decision that you are probably not ready to make. In the meantime, going to college gives you the chance to learn more about yourself and acquire the information that you need so that when you make that decision, as you inevitably will, you will be more prepared.

(3) You will have proved that you are able to finish what you started. Now this is a very important character trait that is highly valued by employers and business associates. If you are hired to do a job, you must be able to finish it. A college degree demonstrates that you have done that.

(4) College is society's way of separating those who are smart from those who are not. It is not a perfect measurement, since many smart people never went to college and many people who are not smart graduate from college. But college gives us knowledge and knowledge makes us smarter. Smart people make smart decisions and if college gives you nothing more than that, then it has given you all that you need.

(5) I'm paying for it, so just go.

It was, of course, the last argument that convinced them. But I hope when their children confront them with their own original objections to college, they will remember my first four points.

Crafting the Summary

The **summary** is the first of the three writing tasks that make up the written response. In it, you are asked to identify *in your own words* the author's main ideas. You are asked to use your own words in order to demonstrate that you understand the passage: If you can explain it in your own way, then you know what it means. Don't include ideas that are *not* in the passage. For example, don't include your own opinions or reflections on the ideas in the passage in this summary. Reserve those for a later section.

Your summary should focus on the main points of the passage. A good rule of thumb is to avoid mentioning dates, statistics, numbers, or names because they are usually used as evidence to support the author's main ideas. Later on, you may want to refer to the supporting details, but the summary should concentrate on the author's main ideas, not the details that support them.

For example, in the lottery passage, you should avoid mentioning the financing of the Jamestown settlement in 1612 by the English government. This is evidence that supports the key point that the lottery has played an important role in American history because it generates income for government operations and projects.

Transfer this information onto scrap paper in the form of a bulleted list or an outline, starting at the beginning of the passage and moving through to the end. Your list should consist of no more than four or five items. Write out each of these key points as a complete sentence, and put them in the order in which they were in the reading passage. A list for the reading selection on the lottery might look something like this:

> ✔ *The lottery has played an important role in the history of America by the way it generates income for government operations and projects.*
>
> ✔ *The lottery makes no sense economically for those who play it because of the outrageous odds of winning.*
>
> ✔ *It does possess value as a form of entertainment because it creates fantasies, hopes, drama, and dreams.*
>
> ✔ *The only winner in the lottery is the government.*
>
> ✔ *The lottery agencies need to be held accountable for where the money goes and why the success rate is so low.*

Notice that the language in the list is different from the language in the reading selection. The summary needs to be *in your own words*. This means that you cannot merely quote from the reading passage or even just substitute synonyms (words that mean the same thing) for words in the passage. Relying on the language of the passage—even if you put those words in quotation marks—will suggest that you do not truly understand it.

Include the author's name and the title of the reading selection in your summary to signal to the reader that the information you are conveying comes from the reading passage, and add transitional words and phrases, such as *because, although,* and *for example,* to make the connections between ideas clear to your reader.

Once you have written your summary, read it over. Think of yourself as a reviewer telling a reader (in this case, the grader) what the original passage is about. You are preparing your reader so that he or she can understand the analysis you will present later.

With all these tips in mind, compare the effective summary paragraph on the left, constructed from the bullet list above, with the faulty summary paragraph on the right:

	Effective Summary	Faulty Summary	
Author, title	In the "The Lottery Is for Losers" by Mary Pickford, the author claims that lottery agencies should be made to explain how money generated by the lottery gets spent and why so few people who play the lottery actually win. The lottery has played an important role in the development of America because it is a way of financing public projects. Unfortunately, it is really a very bad investment for those who play it because the odds of winning it are so high. It does have some value for those who play it, but only in the entertainment it provides. The only real financial winner is the government. For this reason, the author believes that the lottery agencies should disclose the realities of the lottery scam, "Who really wins?" the author asks.	In 1892, the Supreme Court banned lotteries, but in 1964, states revived the lottery as a way of generating revenue without raising taxes. The biggest problem with the lottery is that it makes no economic sense to play it, since the odds of winning are 1 in 14–175 million. It makes sense once we recognize its value as entertainment, the thrill of buying the magic tickets and the drama of watching the numbers roll down the chute. The lottery represents the American dream. Isn't it about time the government were held accountable for the realities of their product.	Language from the text
Main claim			
Key supporting point 1			Unnecessary detail
Transition			
Key supporting point 2			
Key supporting point 3			
Key supporting point 4			
Repeats main claim as conclusion			
Quotation			

Notice that the effective paraphrase on the left puts ideas from the passage into original words and sentences, except for one short quotation. Including a brief quotation, while not required, is a nice touch. It demonstrates the writer's ability to judge what kind of a quotation would be appropriate and it demonstrates that the writer knows how to use quotations marks and integrate a quotation into a sentence, without relying too heavily on the language of the passage.

The ineffective summary, in contrast, merely strings together words and phrases from the reading passage, and it includes minor supporting details that are not needed. It would be considered ineffective because the writer has not demonstrated *in his or her own words*, that he or she understands the passage.

When you are ready to write your summary, leave about six lines at the top of the page—you will need this space to insert your introduction later—and then begin writing a summary paragraph based on your list. Your summary will combine these sentences into a paragraph. You may need to add transitional words and phrases, such as *because, although, for example,* and so on.

Now Try It Yourself!

Using your annotations from the passage above (p. 11), write a summary of "Go to College" by Arthur Digby Sellers.

Developing Your Significant Idea

Developing your significant idea is the second task that the writing directions ask you to complete. According to the directions, you must develop your response by focusing on a significant idea from the passage and explaining *why* you think it is significant. Identifying this idea will give you your central focus, or **thesis**, which you will develop in the rest of your response.

Identifying a Significant Idea

At this point, you may be asking yourself how you choose a significant idea to focus on. Try the following:

1. Ask yourself, "Why does the point that the author is making even matter?" In other words, why does the author even consider the idea of the lottery, the way it operates, and who really benefits? Your answer to this question can function as your central focus. It can also lead to an interesting examination that will allow you to use some of the details that the author uses in the passage. After all, you should develop your response by integrating details from the passage into your own response.

2. Choose a key idea from the passage (one of the key ideas in your summary). Many students struggle in their response by choosing an idea that is not supported by the passage. For example, a writer who focused on the lottery as a valuable mechanism that enables poor people to go from rags to riches would probably not get a strong score. Why? Because this is not an idea that can be found in the passage no matter how hard you look for it.

3. Choose an idea that departs from a conventional or ordinary way of thinking. An idea that is obvious states what everyone already knows. You do not need to repeat it. So, for instance, if the idea you choose to focus on is that the lottery is a form of gambling, then you are unlikely to be able to engage the passage at a critically complex or insightful level. If, on the other hand, you say that it is popular even though those who play it are destined to lose, then there is an observation that might raise eyebrows and force you to use your powers of persuasion.

4. Choose an idea, not a fact. Facts, unless they are surprising, are difficult to analyze or argue for or against. They are a dead end. For example, asserting as your significant idea that the odds of winning the lottery are between 14 million to 1 and 175 million to 1 will leave you with nowhere to go. The fact of the odds must be linked to an opinion that is arguable. An effective main idea would claim something based on the facts, that *because* of the ridiculous odds, people must play the lottery for its entertainment or fantasy value. This is an opinion linked to a fact that can be examined. Of course, you can use the author's facts to support your own idea, but the facts themselves should not be your significant idea.

5. Choose an idea that is specific enough that you can explore it thoughtfully and fully in the time allotted and support it with a concrete example. An overly general central focus will be difficult to support with enough detail to make the response compelling. For instance,

the idea that the main function of the lottery is to raise money for government operations is very large and probably too weighty to handle in the short time that you have. But the idea that the government was able to ignore its opposition to gambling and approve the lottery—a form of gambling—anyway is narrower in scope and probably an idea you could examine in ninety minutes.

Once you have chosen a significant idea, go back to your summary and make sure that this idea is included there.

Now Try It Yourself!

Using the steps outlined above, develop a significant idea based on your summary of the reading passage "Go to College" (p. 13). (The reading passage itself appears on p. 11.)

Explaining Its Significance

Once you have chosen a significant idea, you must explain *why* that idea matters. This process is similar to that used by lawyers defending a client:

1. You begin by asserting your claim: "My client is innocent!"

2. You cite the reasons that support your claim: "My client had no motive. He has no police record. He was in Singapore at the time the crime occurred. Another person answering his description is on trial for the same crime."

3. You offer evidence in support of your reasons: The client's nonexistent rap sheet, eye-witness statements from the flight attendant and the other passengers on his trans-Pacific flight, testimony from the police officer who arrested the look-alike.

Like the lawyer, you start with your claim and then make your jury believe the claim by providing logical reasons and persuasive evidence.

Your response should isolate an idea from the passage that you find most compelling, and then develop an extended response to it. You are not yet supporting your idea with evidence—that will come next—so this section of your response should leave out personal references.

Imagine that you are writing a response to "The Lottery Is for Losers." One claim the author makes in passing is that people play the lottery, not to win, but rather to fantasize about winning. This is a potentially significant idea from the reading passage that you could develop because it is the opposite of what one might think. ("How odd!" one might respond. "You mean people don't play to win? Why should I believe that?")

To develop this idea, you might say that most people lead ordinary lives, that they work dull jobs with little hope of change or excitement, that they dream of exchanging their boring lives for the thrilling lives they see in movies and on television. Since they will never earn enough money from their low-paying jobs to realize their dreams, their only escape is into fantasy. The odds of winning the lottery are impossible (1 in 14 million or worse), so most people don't actually believe they'll win. Instead, they ignore the odds and focus on the possibility, dreaming of never again eating beans from a can or buying their clothes off the rack or riding the subway home during rush hour. The whole value of the lottery is in what it promises, not what it delivers.

This, in a nutshell, is the structure of the significant idea paragraph.

Below is a sample central focus (or thesis statement) that highlights this surprising but interesting main idea:

> *In this passage, Pickford makes the interesting point that in spite of the impossible odds of winning the lottery, millions of people continue to spend billions of dollars playing it. Since they are highly unlikely to win—and they know it—people must be playing the lottery for the <u>fantasy</u> of winning.*

Notice how this central focus refers to a significant idea in the reading passage ("In this passage, Pickford makes the interesting point. . . .") and then offers the writer's conclusion.

Now Try It Yourself!

Using the significant idea that you developed above (p. 15), write a thesis statement for your written response to "Go to College."

Supporting the Central Focus with Reasons and Evidence

Once you have identified your significant idea, you will need to develop your central focus into an effective paragraph. While there are many idea-generating techniques available, such as free-writing, brainstorming, asking the journalists' questions (*who, what, where, when, why,* and *how*), and clustering or mapping, you won't have a lot of time during the exam to experiment, so let's work with a **scratch** (or informal) **outline**.

A scratch outline is a useful prewriting activity that allows you to jot down your ideas, moving from one supporting idea to the next.

Starting with the central focus above, let's sketch out a possible journey through a paragraph that explains the idea of winning the lottery as fantasy:

Support (reason)	*Lottery designed for people to lose*
	↓
Support (reason)	*Its purpose is to raise money for government operations*
	↓
Support (fact)	*Astronomical odds: 1 to 175 million at worst!*
	↓
Support (fact)	*No formula for picking numbers works*
	↓
Support (fact)	*Studying past winning numbers doesn't work either*

Central focus	*People play in order to entertain the fantasy of winning*
	↓
Support (fact)	*People have boring jobs*
	↓
Support (fact)	*People have unfulfilling home lives*
	↓
Support (fact)	*People suffer from bad health*
	↓
Support (fact)	*When nothing is going right, people retreat into fantasy*
	↓
Support (fact)	*Playing the lottery requires only a small investment*
	↓
Restatement of central focus	*Playing the lottery is a form of fantasy wish fulfillment*

You may resist the idea of creating a scratch outline because you may think that it will take too long and that it is unnecessary, but a two-minute investment may save you time and frustration later. Now let's build the paragraph from the scratch outline above.

The lottery is, in fact, designed for people to lose. After all, its primary function is to raise revenue for government operations, not to make people rich. It is not impossible to win, but the odds are astronomical: At worst, it's 1 chance in 175 million! Players have a better chance of being hit by lightning. Besides, no one can select the winning numbers by a formula or by studying past winning numbers. So a realistic hope of winning can't be what drives people to continue playing the lottery. It must be something else, something more powerful than greed. I think it is fantasy. People's jobs and personal lives may be unfulfilling and their health may be falling apart, but the lottery still provides them with a satisfying fantasy. The smallest investment — "A dollar and a dream" as the slogan for the New York State lottery has it — gives players many hours of pleasure as they fantasize about how winning the lottery would change their lives.

Central Focus (label pointing to: "So a realistic hope of winning can't be what drives people to continue playing the lottery. It must be something else, something more powerful than greed. I think it is fantasy.")

Restatement of Central Focus (in different words) (label pointing to: "The smallest investment — "A dollar and a dream" as the slogan for the New York State lottery has it — gives players many hours of pleasure as they fantasize about how winning the lottery would change their lives.")

You build your paragraph from the scratch outline above, adding information as you move forward, but remaining faithful to your scratch outline. Ending your paragraph with a restatement of your central focus, in different words, provides a neat way to give your paragraph closure and remind readers of your central idea as you move forward into the supporting paragraph.

Now Try It Yourself!

Build a central-idea paragraph based on the central-idea statement (thesis) that you devised at the end of the previous section. Try creating a scratch outline before you write your paragraph.

Supporting Your Claims with Evidence and Examples

The third writing task asks you to support your significant idea with evidence or examples drawn from your reading, your schoolwork, or your personal experience. An effective supporting paragraph will begin with a topic, or main idea, sentence that supports your thesis statement by providing concrete supporting evidence or examples. Consider the following topic sentence:

I have witnessed firsthand the power of the lottery to create a fantasy.

This topic sentence carries forward the idea introduced and developed in the previous paragraph of the fantasy element that dominates the mentality of those who play the lottery.

The most important consideration is that the evidence or examples need to be relevant to the significant idea. Below is a scratch outline for a paragraph that supports the main idea using a personal example:

- *An old man I used to work with*
  ↓
  Used to talk about sunny beaches, expensive cars, pretty girls
  ↓
  Learned a lot about the lottery from this old man
  ↓
- *Lottery created the worst kind of dependencies*
  ↓
  Encourages people to underestimate the responsibilities that make life worth living
  ↓
  Family, work, learning
  ↓
- *Create fantasies that substitute what's silly and selfish for what's important*
  ↓
  Imagining a dream landscape that is unrealistic and out of character

Working from the scratch outline, let's construct a paragraph that supports the topic sentence above.

> *Some old guy I used to work with would talk about sunny beaches, expensive cars, and pretty girls. When I asked him how he expected to get these things, he said, as if it were the most natural thing in the world, the lottery. I learned a lot about the lottery from this old man. I realized from his ridiculous fantasies that the lottery creates the worst kinds of dependencies. It encourages people to underestimate the important things in life—work, family, leisure, learning—and substitute for them a silly and fictitious dream landscape. And even if you had the chance to enjoy the things that you think you want, how long would it be before you realize that you don't really want them after all because you wanted other things or even newer things?*

Using Examples from Your Coursework or Reading

According to the writing directions, your support section can come from your reading, from your coursework, or from something that you have experienced personally. These directions are not intended to indicate an order of preference, but because most students tend to rely on personal examples, support drawn from your coursework or reading stands out. Remember that the scorers who will be grading your exam are English professors, instructors of writing or literature. In addition to well-crafted personal experiences, English professors appreciate essays that make reference to literary texts or ideas that originate in academic courses because the evidence or example can be verified. Examples that refer to a friend, a relative, or oneself, like the one on page 18, are permissible, but they can sometimes seem fake; the personal example works only if it can be believed. Compare these two supporting paragraphs, one based on something learned in class and another based on something read:

Paragraph Based on Something Learned in a Class	Paragraph Based on Something Read
My own sense of the silliness of the lottery comes from what I learned about gambling in psychology class. Any way you look at it, the lottery is a game of chance. It may be legal and it may even help the government, but that doesn't change the fact that it deceives people by giving them a false sense of security. Any gambler will tell you that the bet he places represents one outcome out of many possible outcomes. "This will happen instead of all these other things," he seems to be saying. Of course, some outcomes are unlikely, but others are just as possible as the one the gambler bets on. The gambler may think that his choice is an intelligent one, one that seems most probable. It might be one horse out of a field of eight, or one team over another team, or one series of numbers instead of another series of numbers. But anything can happen once the gambler's bet is in. And if the	When I think of the confusion that people have about why they play the lottery, I think of the short story "The Lottery" by Shirley Jackson. In her story, the people of the community conduct an annual lottery which everybody plays. The problem is that no one remembers why they carry on the tradition of drawing lots, and they have even forgotten the details of the history of the black box from which they draw their pieces of paper. But is this any different from the lottery that millions of people play today? They think they're playing in order to win, but they know they never will because the odds make it next to impossible. They think that when they win they'll move to the Caribbean and fish all day. The truth is most winners never even quit their jobs. The real reason they play, the one they never even think about, is the fantasy of winning. For most people who play the lottery, the winning takes place between the

gambler thinks that his bet controlled the outcome, or that the outcome was inevitable, then the gambler just doesn't understand the way reality works. It's all just dumb luck.	purchase of the tickets and the drawing of the numbers. Most of them don't even know why they play.

Both paragraphs carry forward the essay's central focus developed in the previous paragraph. The paragraph on the left, based on something learned in a psychology class, argues that the one who plays the lottery is under a misconception regarding the nature of gambling. The gambler may think he or she is picking the right combination of numbers, numbers that make sense, but it is all fantasy and chance. The gambler does not control the outcome. The paragraph on the right is based on something read, Shirley Jackson's famous story "The Lottery." The connection that the writer makes between this story and the fantasy and entertainment value of lottery play in our current society also develops the central focus that people are not really aware of why they do things. Since the writing task encourages you to use information from your coursework or your readings, you should feel free to go in either of those directions.

Now Try It Yourself!

Craft a paragraph providing concrete facts or logical reasons to support the central-idea paragraph you drafted at the end of the previous section (p. 17). Try creating a scratch outline before you write your paragraph.

Writing the Conclusion and Introduction

A CATW response that begins with the summary, moves to the significant idea, and concludes with the example can receive a passing score, but it will not likely receive much more than a middle-range score. Responses that score in the upper range provide a little more than what is asked for in the directions. In order to receive an upper-range score, your response should have an introduction and a conclusion. Adding an introduction and a conclusion demonstrates understanding of coherent essay structure, and that is what graders like to see.

Writing the Conclusion

An effective conclusion should be short and to the point (no more than three or four sentences), it should refer back to the significant idea, and it should indicate why this idea is important. Here is an example of an effective concluding paragraph:

> *There is a good reason why the lottery makes as much money as it does. Especially in difficult economic times, people will always turn to the lottery for the dream of wealth they can't realize in their ordinary lives. Unfortunately, it doesn't work because life just doesn't work that way. It's a game for losers. The only way to win at the lottery is to take your lottery ticket money and spend it on something else.*

This conclusion is effective because it refers back to the idea that playing the lottery is about fantasy, and it indicates why this idea is important, showing that by living this fantasy, lottery ticket buyers lose something very real: their money.

Now Try It Yourself!

Craft a conclusion to accompany the central-idea and supporting-idea paragraphs that you have already written (pp. 17, 20). Make sure that it refers back to your significant idea and shows why that idea is important.

Writing the Introduction

The introduction should probably be the last section you write, since your central focus will not fully emerge until you complete the significant idea and support sections of the response. Your introduction should introduce your summary of the reading passage, so you might mention a key term, idea, or person from the passage. It should also prepare the reader for your significant idea. Some strategies for introducing your significant idea in the introduction include the following:

- Concentrate on conditions that make your central focus possible: "Because of *the current high rate of unemployment*, people have turned to the lottery as an alternative source of income. They are willing to believe that they are able to beat the odds and win the money that they need to support their families."

- Discuss the historical situation that has led to the problems suggested by your central focus: "*America's cities have always depended upon income from the lottery to finance its operations.* Sadly, this dependence on the lottery has led some cities to overlook the fact that many who play the lottery become hooked."

- Call attention to a looming disaster that makes it essential that we begin to pay attention to the threat implied by the central focus: "The lottery is a game that promises those who play the opportunity to win enormous amounts of money, but it rarely fulfills that promise. In this time of economic struggle for many, *the lottery is an even bigger temptation* than it is in times of prosperity."

- Emphasize a psychological fact of life that makes the central focus a condition that needs to be addressed: "The astronomical odds of winning the lottery make it painfully clear that people continue to play, not because they have a realistic chance of winning, but rather because *they enjoy the fantasy of winning*. People who play the lottery need to understand why they do what they do."

Here is a sample introduction:

<table>
<tr>
<td>Explains lottery's appeal</td>
<td>*If you have ever imagined exchanging the life you have for the life you have always dreamed of having, at some point you have played the <u>lottery</u>.* If you are lucky, or smart, you played it once or twice, realized that there is no way to win it, and turned to some other, perhaps surer, method of making your</td>
</tr>
<tr>
<td>Key terms</td>
<td>dreams come true. Then there are those for whom the <u>lottery</u> dream never dies.</td>
</tr>
</table>

Now Try It Yourself!

Craft an introduction to accompany the central-idea, supporting-idea, and concluding paragraphs you have already written (pp. 17, 20, 21). Make sure that your introduction prepares the reader for your significant idea.

Crafting the Finished Product

Now let's put all the parts together and see how it looks.

Sample Response

If you have ever imagined exchanging the life you have for the life you have always dreamed of having, at some point you have played the lottery. If you are lucky, or smart, you played it once or twice, realized that there is no way to win it, and turned to some other, perhaps surer, method of making your dreams come true. Then there are those for whom the lottery dream never dies.

In "The Lottery Is for Losers" by Mary Pickford, the author claims that lottery agencies should be made to explain why so few people who play the lottery actually win and where all the money actually goes. The lottery has played an important role in the development of America because it is a way of financing public projects. Unfortunately, it is really a very bad investment for those who play it because the odds against winning it are so high. It does have some value for those who play it, but only in the entertainment it provides. The only real financial winner is the government. For this reason, the author believes that the lottery agencies should disclose the realities of the lottery scam, "Who really wins?" the author asks.

In this passage, the author makes the interesting point that in spite of the impossible odds of winning the lottery, millions of people continue to spend billions of dollars playing it. Since they are highly unlikely to win—and they know it—people must be playing the lottery for the <u>fantasy</u> of winning. The lottery is, in fact, designed for people to lose. After all, its primary function is to raise revenue for government operations, not make people rich. It is not impossible to win, but the odds against it are astronomical. You have a better chance of being hit by lightning. Besides, no one can select the winning numbers by a mathematical process such as a formula or by studying past winning numbers. Something else drives people to continue playing the lottery, something more powerful than greed. I think it is fantasy. When your job, if you even have one, or your personal life, or your health are all unfulfilling or falling apart, there's still the fantasy of a dream come true that is possible if you can just pick the right numbers. When nothing else seems to be going right, there's always the fantasy that with the smallest investment you can turn it around by winning the lottery jackpot. In other words, what we call addiction to the lottery is nothing more than a show of faith, or insanity, since it always produces the same results.

I have witnessed firsthand the power and danger of lottery fever by seeing how it contributes to a lifetime of fantasy. Some old guy I used to work with would talk about sunny beaches, expensive cars, and pretty girls. When I asked him how he expected to get these things since he never had any money, he said, as if it was the most natural thing in the world, the lottery. I learned a lot about the lottery from this old man. I realized from his ridiculous fantasies that the lottery creates the worst kinds of dependencies. It encourages people to devalue the important things in life—work, family, leisure, learning—and substitute for them a silly and fictitious dream landscape, wasting lots of money in the process. And even if you had the chance to enjoy the things that you think you want, how long would it be before they would begin to bore you to tears, before you wanted other things, new things?

There is a good reason why the lottery makes as much money as it does. Especially in difficult economic times, people will always turn to the lottery for the dream of wealth they can't realize in their ordinary lives. Unfortunately, it doesn't work because life just doesn't work that way. It's a game for suckers. The only way to win at the lottery is to take your lottery ticket money and spend it on something else.

Now Try It Yourself!

Put all the pieces together, and congratulate yourself. You have now written a practice response that will help you succeed on the CATW. Read through it to see how well you like the results!

Editing and Proofreading

There is one last—but certainly not the least—important part to the writing process: editing and proofreading your work. Dedicate ten to fifteen minutes to this process. As you read your draft, look for places where you may need to clarify or explain a point or add support to an underdeveloped passage. Make sure that you have not left out any words. And look out for errors in sentence structure (Have you corrected sentence fragments, comma splices, and run-on sentences?), punctuation (Have you used commas correctly?), and verb and noun endings (Have you checked to make sure that your subjects and verbs match in number and gender?). Finally, proofread your response to make sure that words are spelled correctly and that you haven't confused any words (such as *it's*, a contraction of *it is*, for *its*, the possessive pronoun—*its* left paw is hurt). For more about editing and proofreading, see chapter 5.

Now Try It Yourself!

Using the information in chapter 5, edit and proofread your written response. Make sure to check that your ideas are clear and fully developed and that you have avoided problems with sentence structure, grammar, punctuation, and spelling.

4 Taking the Exam: Writing Your Own Response

In the previous chapter, we looked at how to unpack the passage and then construct a response. In this chapter, you will unpack a passage yourself and construct your own response. As you work through your written response, you may want to refer to the previous chapter for guidance.

Begin by reading the following passage entitled "Columbus." As you read it through the first time, pay attention to the writer's main ideas.

Columbus
by John Barrymore

The description of any historical event represents the point of view of the historian. The history may claim to tell the truth, but in the end all you really get is one version of what happened. Since any point of view is the product of specific biases—religious, cultural, ideological, gender, sexual—the description of the events from that point of view will naturally be distorted by those biases. When the truth is unavailable, the best we can hope for is a good story. Consider, for example, two of the many competing stories of the exploits of Christopher Columbus.

There is the figure of Christopher Columbus that emerges from the pages of the many textbooks used in America's public schools. In this version, the heroic Italian seaman and explorer receives support from Queen Isabella of Spain in 1492 in order to discover a shorter passage to India, which would give Spain entry into the lucrative spice and silk trade with Asia. With three ships under his command, he instead discovers America and the islands of the Caribbean, proves that the earth is round, and returns to Spain with a fortune in gold. He convinces Isabella to fund three more voyages, marking the beginning of the European colonization of the New World.

Then there is the version that portrays Columbus from a less flattering angle. Like most informed people of his day, Columbus already knows the earth is round. If he sails west, he will eventually arrive in the Far East. But when he stumbles upon the islands of the Caribbean, he realizes he has discovered land unknown to earlier European explorers. He notices that the gentle natives display gold trinkets and gold masks and Columbus changes his plans. He establishes an extensive network of slave labor camps on the different islands for the purpose of mining gold and other precious metals. Soon, he returns to Spain with a huge fortune in gold and about 500 slaves, half of whom die on the way. He promises Isabella even greater riches and more slaves if she will give him additional ships and men. Within two years of Columbus's arrival in the New World, half of the 250,000 Indians on Haiti are dead from the conditions in the mines and, according to Las Casas, Columbus's chronicler, between 1494 and 1508, 3 million Caribbean natives perish from starvation and brutality. In fact, in 1500, Columbus is arrested and returned to Spain to stand trial for acts of cruelty. It is worth noting that the man who is credited with discovering America never even set foot on any part of the United States.

There are infinite versions of the Columbus story. In some he is a hero; in others he is a villain. It depends on who tells the story and why. After all, every storyteller has a motive that has nothing to do with explaining what really happened. But if the truth is unknowable, then it is secondary. What is more valuable for us is which version is the most compelling.

Crafting the Summary

Read the passage a second time. This time, underline or note in the margin the places in the text where the author states his main ideas. List the four or five (you should not have more than five) main ideas below. Make sure you put them in complete sentences and use your own words.

- _____

- _____

- _____

- _____

- _____

Craft your summary paragraph using the list above. As you do so, be aware of the importance of creating connections among your sentences. Use transition words such as *since, because,* or *although.* If the sentences lack connection, the paragraph will seem choppy and disconnected. Also, remember to include the title of the passage and the name of the author.

Summary:

_____

_____

_____

_____

_____

Developing Your Significant Idea

Now that you have written your summary paragraph, move on to the second writing task: Write down the idea that you feel is most significant or most interesting from the reading passage and briefly explain its significance.

Identifying the Significant Idea and Explaining Its Significance

To identify your significant idea, start by asking yourself, "Why does the point that author is making even matter?" Then choose a key idea from the passage (one of the key ideas in your summary), or an idea in the passage that departs from a conventional or ordinary way of thinking. It should be an idea that is specific enough so that you can explore it thoughtfully and fully with a concrete example. Finally, make sure it is an idea that reasonable people could disagree about, not a fact (something that is either true or false).

The idea in the passage that I find most interesting is:

_____

_____

_____

_____

Now write a sentence or two explaining *why* this idea is interesting or important.
I find this idea interesting because:

_____

_____

_____

_____

This significant or interesting idea will serve as the central focus of your response.

Supporting the Central Focus with Reasons and Evidence

Now that you have explained why your idea is interesting or important, create a scratch outline, listing the reasons and evidence that will persuade others to agree with you:

Key supporting idea(s) _____

↓

Support (reason/evidence) _____

↓

Support (reason/evidence) _____

↓

Support (reason/evidence) _____

↓

Support (reason/evidence) _____

↓

Support (reason/evidence) _____

↓

Support (reason/evidence) _____

↓

Support (reason/evidence) _____

Using the reasons and evidence in the scratch outline above, construct a paragraph explaining why your idea is significant or interesting:

_____

_____

_____

_____

_____

_____

_____

_____

_____

_____

_____

_____

_____

Remember: Ending your paragraph with a restatement of your central focus, in different words, provides closure and reminds readers of your central idea as you move forward into the supporting paragraph.

Supporting Your Claims with Evidence and Examples

The next section addresses the third writing task. You need to support your significant or interesting idea by giving an example or providing evidence from your reading, from your schoolwork, or from something that you have personally experienced. Think of your example or your evidence as making your significant or interesting idea real for the reader. For instance, to make the problem of overcrowding in the subway real for readers, you could describe the experience of being crushed in a subway car during rush hour.

Start the paragraph by writing a topic sentence that identifies your example and explains its relationship to the significant idea:

_____

_____

Now develop a paragraph from this topic sentence by expanding the connection or the association between your significant idea and your example. If you are writing a descriptive paragraph, you might provide additional details about what the experience felt like or looked like to develop your paragraph. If you are using narration (telling a story), tell what happened next, choosing events that help support your main idea. If you are using a comparison to develop your paragraph, explain how something you learned, read about, or experienced was like or unlike what you discussed in your topic sentence.

For instance, using the example of the overcrowded subway, a descriptive paragraph might focus on how it felt to be crushed in the middle of the car as more and more riders poured onto the train. A narrative paragraph might tell the story of fighting your way to the door as you tried to exit. A comparative paragraph might compare the experience of riding the subway in New York with riding the subway in Washington, D.C.

An effective paragraph will do three things:

- It will provide a clear topic sentence linking the supporting description, story, or comparison to the significant idea.

- It will provide evidence that supports the topic sentence.

- It will provide a concluding sentence that reminds readers of the connection to the significant idea and prepares them to move on to the conclusion.

Keeping in mind the connection between your significant idea and the example that represents it, create a scratch outline for your paragraph:

Topic sentence (must support thesis)

• _____

↓

_____

↓

_____

↓

_____

Support (description, narration, comparison, etc.)

_____

↓

_____

↓

_____

Concluding sentence (connects support to thesis/ significant idea)

• _____

_____

_____

Using the reasons and evidence in the scratch outline on the previous page, construct a paragraph that provides a description, story, comparison, or something else that supports your significant or interesting idea:

_____

_____

_____

_____

_____

_____

_____

_____

_____

Be sure you use transition words and phrases to make the connections between your sentences clear to your reader.

Writing the Conclusion and Introduction

The last two parts you will write are a short conclusion and a short introduction. The conclusion will restate the response's interesting or significant idea, that is, your response's central focus. The introduction will prepare the reader for your interesting or significant idea.

Review the topic sentence you wrote for your significant-idea paragraph, and revise it as a conclusion. Remember, you have proven this idea by developing and explaining it in the second writing task and by supporting your claim with evidence or an example in the third writing task.

Conclusion:

_____

_____

_____

_____

_____

_____

_____

Your introduction should hint at your significant or interesting idea, preparing the reader for what is to come. This will be the last section that you write since you will not know what your significant idea is until you identify it through writing the summary.

Introduction:

_____

_____

_____

_____

_____

_____

Crafting the Finished Product

You're finished, almost. All you have to do is put the pieces together, read them through to make sure that what you have written is clear, and then proofread your response to correct any errors in grammar, punctuation, or spelling. Editing and proofreading are so important that they deserve their own chapter, so read chapter 5 before returning to edit and proofread your response.

Now Try It Yourself!

Trade drafts with a classmate. Read your classmate's response and consider his or her significant idea and the reasons and evidence your classmate provides. Restate the writer's thesis in your own words. Now outline your classmate's response. Is the response logically organized? Does it follow the structure discussed above (introduction, summary of the reading passage, statement of the significant idea, explanation of the significant idea, evidence supporting the significant idea, and brief conclusion)? If not, does it include all of the parts in an order that makes sense to you?

Now Try It Yourself!

Once you have reviewed a classmate's written response, evaluate your own response. Make whatever changes you think are needed to create an effective summary, a clear statement of your significant idea, a logical explanation of why your significant idea matters or is important, effective evidence supporting your significant idea, and a brief introduction and conclusion.

5 Editing and Proofreading

You may have composed your response carefully, but *no one* is perfect. Even the best writers repeat themselves, say something in a roundabout way, leave words out, omit verb endings, and misspell words. All writers could find better ways to phrase something the second or third time through the response. So be sure to edit and proofread your work before handing it in.

Read your response twice. The first time through, read to determine that what you have written will be clear to your reader.

- Have you included the author's name and the title of the reading passage in your summary?

- Do your paragraphs have topic sentences?

- Does your supporting paragraph (or paragraphs) relate directly to your significant idea?

- Have you chosen the most specific word(s) possible? A word like *individual* sounds overly general in comparison with a description—*a tiny boy in a red baseball cap* or *the scrawny old man in his ratty sweater and filthy work pants.*

- Is anything missing, such as words, phrases, or supporting examples? You can always insert words, sentences, even whole paragraphs, in the margins or on the unlined pages of the test booklet. It is more important to say what has to be said than not to say it because you may be worried about how sloppy the writing will look. You are not being graded for neatness. If the information is in the test booklet, it will be read by the grader in the order that you indicate that it is to be read.

Once you have made changes to the content, read the response again to eliminate repetition and wordiness.

- Eliminate information that is repeated unnecessarily.

- Eliminate wordy phrases such as *at the present time* (replace with *today*), *due to the fact that* (replace with *because*), and *in spite of the fact that* (replace with *although*).

- Eliminate empty modifiers, such as *absolutely, literally, really,* and *very.*

- Eliminate redundant words:

Raced already conveys the idea "with speed," so *quickly* is redundant

➤ Eleanor ~~quickly~~ raced down a ~~thronged and~~ crowded Fifth Avenue.

Thronged and *crowded* mean the same thing, so only one is needed.

Finally, read your response, checking for errors of grammar, punctuation, and spelling. Here are some tips to help you proofread your work more effectively:

- As you read, touch each word with the tip of your finger. This forces you to slow down and, more importantly, to see and read what is on the page instead of what you think is on the page. If you read too fast, you will not see what you have left out. Touch each word.

- Read your response to yourself silently but listen to it with your "mind's ear," as if you were reading it aloud to a friend. (You do not want to disturb the person sitting next to you.)

- Look for missing punctuation marks, such as commas and periods. (See chapter 8 for more about using commas.) Use your dictionary to look up any words that seem to be misspelled. Look for missing verb endings, such as *-ed*, *-ing*, and *-s* or *-es*. Make sure your subjects and verbs agree. (See chapter 8 for more about subject-verb agreement.) Check to make sure that each sentence has a subject and a verb and that you have not created any sentence fragments, run-on sentences, or comma splices. Finally, look for the kinds of errors that your instructor has marked on your previous work. (See chapter 8 for more about sentence fragments, run-on sentences, and comma splices.)

Now Try It Yourself!

Edit the passage below to eliminate wordiness and repetition. There are many ways to eliminate wordiness, but one possible "answer" appears on page 67.

> The lottery is, as a matter of fact, designed for people to lose. After all, its first and primary function is absolutely to raise revenue dollars for government operations, not to make certain people literally very rich. It is not absolutely impossible to end up winning, but the odds against winning are astronomically high: At worst, it's 1 chance in 175 million! The people who play the lottery have a better chance of being hit by lightning.

Now Try It Yourself!

Edit and proofread the following paragraph. Read the passage twice. The first time through, read to determine whether the paragraph will be clear to a reader, and add information where it is missing. The second time through, correct any errors in grammar, punctuation, and spelling. As you read the passage a second time, touch each word and "listen" as you read the response silently to yourself. Look for missing or unnecessary punctuation marks. Add verb endings and noun endings where they are required. Correct misspellings. Repair errors in sentence structure. See if you can locate where the first paragraph ends and the second one begins.

> I relize that many student at New York community collage hardly seem to want a education, there here becuase its better then the other options. Maybe there parents wanted them to go to collage just to get them outta the house. Maybe they're friends are at the school and they just wanna hang out. Maybe its just there way of put off having to go to work full time. Most of these student actually go to there classes, but many are not involve and just sit in the back of the classroom and text messege on their phones, they just come an put in an appearance thought they don't have any committment to there work, this kinds of student dont do much for the collage and do less for thereselfs. I spose there must be other resons for student been at New York community collage, but for most student its got more to do with the diploma then the learning. I myself am here partly for the diploma but mostly for the education, I now what I need to do because I been told by my teachers and parnets that you cant get nowhere in life if you dont got a education. I wasted enuff time all ready, Im going to try very hard to get everything I can out of collage, I may never have another chanse to go to school full time again I am going to make the most of this oppertunity.

A corrected version of this passage appears on page 67.

Now Try It Yourself!

Using the methods discussed in the "Now Try It Yourself!" exercise above, edit and proofread the following paragraph.

> There is at least three good reasons why young childern shouldnt watch more then a hour of television a day. First place a limitation on childrens television watching habbits would inable a child to explore other activities that they would'nt even know about if they spent to much time starring at the television. For instance the child could spend more time outside exploring nature first-hand and gets lots of exercise at the same time. And all the books they could read and learn from. Second watching television was a very isolating experience, even when there was other children present, a child would have more friends and know them better if they were able to inneract with each other instead of everyone focusing on the television screen. Finaly children will better enjoy the shows they do watch and learning to be more careful in their choice of programs. This is especially important since they like all of us will almost certainly be life-long television viewers they will either benifit or suffer from there viewing habits, after all we dont allow children only to eat junk food, so why allow them to digest unlimited amounts of televised junk.

A corrected version of this passage appears on page 67.

Now Try It Yourself!

Trade your draft response with a classmate. Using the methods discussed above, edit and proofread your classmate's response. When you are both finished, exchange responses and review the errors your classmate marked. Did he or she catch errors you missed? If so, list those and look out for them in your next sample response or on your CATW.

Now Try It Yourself!

Using the methods discussed above, edit and proofread the response you drafted in chapter 4.

6 Sample Responses with Scores

Below are sample responses and the scores that they would receive from certified CATW scorers across the five areas of assessment. A brief explanation using the scoring rubric follows each score. Keep in mind that these responses are only examples. Many different types of responses could receive the same score.

The responses are based on the selection "Columbus" in chapter 4. Compare the response you drafted in chapter 4 with the samples below. The original reading selection has been repeated here for your convenience.

Columbus
by John Barrymore

The description of any historical event represents the point of view of the historian. The history may claim to tell the truth, but in the end all you really get is one version of what happened. Since any point of view is the product of specific biases—religious, cultural, ideological, gender, sexual—the description of the events from that point of view will naturally be distorted by those biases. When the truth is unavailable, the best we can hope for is a good story. Consider, for example, two of the many competing stories of the exploits of Christopher Columbus.

There is the figure of Christopher Columbus that emerges from the pages of the many textbooks used in America's public schools. In this version, the heroic Italian seaman and explorer receives support from Queen Isabella of Spain in 1492 in order to discover a shorter passage to India, which would give Spain entry into the lucrative spice and silk trade with Asia. With three ships under his command, he instead discovers America and the islands of the Caribbean, proves that the earth is round, and returns to Spain with a fortune in gold. He convinces Isabella to fund three more voyages, marking the beginning of the European colonization of the New World.

Then there is the version that portrays Columbus from a less flattering angle. Like most informed people of his day, Columbus already knows the earth is round. If he sails west, he will eventually arrive in the Far East. But when he stumbles upon the islands of the Caribbean, he realizes he has discovered land unknown to earlier European explorers. He notices that the gentle natives display gold trinkets and gold masks and Columbus changes his plans. He establishes an extensive network of slave labor camps on the different islands for the purpose of mining gold and other precious metals. Soon, he returns to Spain with a huge fortune in gold and about 500 slaves, half of whom die on the way. He promises Isabella even greater riches and more slaves if she will give him additional ships and men. Within two years of Columbus's arrival in the New World, half of the 250,000 Indians on Haiti are dead from the conditions in the mines and, according to Las Casas, Columbus's chronicler, between 1494 and 1508, 3 million Caribbean natives perish from starvation and brutality. In fact, in 1500, Columbus is arrested and returned to Spain to stand trial for acts of cruelty. It is worth noting that the man who is credited with discovering America never even set foot on any part of the United States.

Sample Responses with Scores **39**

There are infinite versions of the Columbus story. In some he is a hero; in others he is a villain. It depends on who tells the story and why. After all, every storyteller has a motive that has nothing to do with explaining what really happened. But if the truth is unknowable, then it is secondary. What is more valuable for us is which version is the most compelling.

WRITING DIRECTIONS

Read the passage above and write an essay responding to the ideas it presents. In your essay, be sure to summarize the passage in your own words, stating the author's most important ideas. Develop your essay by identifying one idea in the passage that you feel is especially significant, and explain its significance. Support your claims with evidence or examples drawn from what you have read, learned in school, and/or personally experienced.

Remember to review your essay and make any changes or corrections that are needed to help your reader follow your thinking. You will have 90 minutes to complete your essay.

Sample Response with Scores of 6 in All Domains

We are told when we are young that the histories that we learn in school and read in the textbooks are the truth, that what we are getting is what really happened. It is not until we get older and read or hear about other versions of those same events that we realize that there are other versions, other truths.

In "Columbus," the author, John Barrymore, argues that the version of a historical event that gets told is the one that makes the best story. It has nothing to do with truth. There are things that get in the way of every story—the author calls them biases—that cause the story to become distorted. Since every story is distorted, the truth cannot be told. It is unavailable in the story. What becomes available to us is, hopefully, a good story. The author uses the example of the story of Christopher Columbus. In the competing histories, he is either a hero or a scoundrel. The version we choose to believe is the one that is most compelling.

What I find most significant is that history is less interested in telling the truth than in telling a good story. It says something about what we prefer to know and believe. As children, we listen to our parents and our teachers and we believe what they tell us. We can't imagine that they would lie. But when we get older, we hear other versions that challenge the earlier versions and we are asked to choose. Of course, we can't choose between the original story that describes acts of heroism and courage and the later story that corrects it with a more "adult" or mature version of evil and treachery. We are already infected by the original candy coated version. What we end up doing is creating our own version of what happened that combines the earlier and the later versions. It has nothing to do with truth but what we prefer to believe because it's a good story.

The author gives the example of Christopher Columbus, but there are countless other examples. I am reminded of the stories I was told when I was young about the settling of the American West. I used to watch westerns with my father and he would insist that John Wayne and the other actors were portrayals of pioneers who singlehandedly defeated the savage Indians and tamed the American frontier. I believed in the heroic figure of John Wayne, saber held high, leading the charge against the painted Indians. When I got older and took a film course in high school, I learned that the American westward migration was nothing like how I had been lead to believe by the movies and especially by my father. The competing version, the one not shown in the movies, was of the hardy pioneers struggling against the hardships of nature and of the noble Indians, anything but savage and violent, displaced by the military into reservations according to the doctrine of Manifest Destiny. The movies never told this story. I still love westerns, and John Wayne is still one of my favorite actors, but my sense of the truth of the events depicted in the movies has, unfortunately, been undermined by another version of the story. I still don't know what is true, but I do know which one I prefer.

At the end of a John Ford movie, "The Man Who Shot Liberty Valance," after the newspaper man has listened to Jimmy Stewart's version of what "really" happened, the newspaper man crumples up his notes and throws them into the fire. He then delivers the famous line: "When legend becomes fact, print the legend." This quote sums up beautifully what the author of "Columbus" is arguing. We love our heroes but we have to create them first. Allegiance to the truth should never get in the way of belief in our hero or the legend that surrounds him or her.

CRITICAL RESPONSE TO TASK AND TEXT: 6

The writer demonstrates an understanding of the complexities of the passage and demonstrates that understanding through the three writing tasks. The writer connects the main ideas in the passage to his own ideas and experiences in a way that is insightful and thoughtful.

DEVELOPMENT: 6

Details and ideas from the passage are skillfully and effectively used to support the writer's own ideas by means of summary, analysis, and narration.

STRUCTURE OF RESPONSE: 6

The writer's response demonstrates a sophisticated awareness of coherent essay structure as it advances through the different writing tasks. The progression or movement of ideas throughout the essay supports the writer's central focus (". . . history is less interested in telling the truth than in telling a good story.").

SENTENCE AND WORD CHOICE: 6

The writer's sentences are effectively controlled and word choice is precise and sophisticated. The writer demonstrates an understanding that sentence variety and vocabulary are stylistic choices that can enhance meaning.

GRAMMAR, USAGE, AND MECHANICS: 6

The precision of the writer's response demonstrates strong command of the rules of composition. Grammar, usage, and mechanics are almost always correct.

The problem with human history is that it is written by human beings. Even when we try to tell the truth about a historical event or person, or attempt to explain what happened or who did it, things get in the way. The biggest obstacle to truth is our need to create heroes and villains.

In "Columbus," John Barrymore explains that every description or explanation of a historical event represents a point of view. Because writers of history are subject to influences, then their points of view are going to be distorted and therefore limited. Even if we try to tell the truth, even if we want to get it right, we will leave things out, put things in, or exaggerate. The truth gets lost but if we're lucky at least we find a good story. The history of Columbus is a perfect example of how our desire for a compelling story results in historical misrepresentations. The truth gets lost, but look closely and you'll find a hero or a scoundrel, maybe both.

Heroes, of course, do not exist if there is no historian or storyteller to create them. This is interesting because if it takes a storyteller to create a hero, then the hero must be a character of fiction. Why else do we write and study history but to give people and events an attractive shape that they do not otherwise possess. Consider the story of Columbus, for example. Let's pretend for a moment that the voyages of Columbus were lost to history and that no record existed to remember him and make him available to us six hundred years later. Then you could say that Columbus did not exist. He may have once existed, but if no history is available to recall him, then he is lost. It takes a historian to bring Columbus back to life after he is dead. It is up to the historian to decide what kind of life he lived. Of course, no one is interested in reading about the ordinary events of an ordinary person. We want to read about figures of importance and acts of greatness. In the case of Columbus, what difference does it make that he was probably guilty of atrocities against the Indians? We need a name and a record for whoever it was who discovered America, so if the historian can give us a good story that serves this need, then it only takes a creative effort to turn Columbus from a villain into a saint.

I can think of any number of examples but the one that comes immediately to mind is from the world of sports. I remember how surprised I was to learn that Mickey Mantle was not really the kind of person in his private life that he appeared to be in the sports pages. When I studied his statistics, the career home runs, the MVP awards, the championships with the Yankees, I could only imagine that he was as heroic in his private life as he was in his public life as an athlete. How could someone who hit 536 home runs and entered the Hall of Fame in the first year of his eligibility be an alcoholic and an absentee father? And yet when I read his biography, all the dirty details came out. The great baseball player was just an ordinary man with simple ambitions and common desires. The sports writers had created a hero out of a farm boy from Oklahoma. Who was the real Mickey Mantle? Who can tell, but behind every athlete lurks a hero, or is it the other way around?

Columbus still enjoys a day of his own. The schools, the banks, and the post offices even close in his honor. But if you ask a bank teller or a mail carrier why he gets to take off every second Monday in October, all he will be able to tell you is that it is in honor of the man who discovered America and proved the earth was round.

CRITICAL RESPONSE TO TASK AND TEXT: 5

The response demonstrates a strong understanding of the main ideas in the text and effectively integrates the author's main ideas with the writer's reading and experiences.

DEVELOPMENT: 5

The writer's ideas are well developed through summary, analysis, and narration. The writer integrates details from the text effectively with details from his own experiences.

STRUCTURE OF RESPONSE: 5

The writer's ideas support a clear central focus. The response demonstrates coherent essay structure as it moves through the writing tasks.

SENTENCE AND WORD CHOICE: 5

The writer's sentences are well controlled and word choice is specific and accurate.

GRAMMAR, USAGE, AND MECHANICS: 5

The response indicates that the writer has good command of the rules of essay composition. Grammar, usage, and mechanics are usually clear.

Sample Response with Scores of 4 in All Domains

In "Columbus" the author, John Barrymore, says that historical events are written from the point of view of the historian. As a result, though historians may claim to tell the truth, they end up telling only one version. Various biases such as religious, cultural, and ideological distort the point of view and make the truth unavailable. We get a good story but a good story is not always true.

The idea that I consider most significant is that the author claims that history is really story telling and not the truth. But when we think about how much of our education is based on history, then is amazing to think that what we learn is just good stories. If Columbus did not discover America and prove the earth was round, then how many other things do we learn in school that is also made up. Its possible that the Civil War was fought for other reasons then freeing the slaves or that America didn't really win World War II. We assume that history is the truth but history is just one version of the truth and if that's the case then they are not the truth.

When I was young I remember how we learned that the stories in the bible were true stories. I learned that Adam and Eve lived in the garden of Eden and that Noah built an ark and gathered all the animals. I believed those bible stories and all the others because we were told they happened and that they were the truth. Also I trusted the people who told them to me. But when I got older, I began to realize that there were other theories that explained the creation of the world like evolution and that there could be no way that Noah could have survived a flood and with all those animals. It just could not have happened that way. Nothing happens the way we are told they happened but we believe it because its a good story. Its when we get older that we learn that there are other versions of it that are more the truth.

So Columbus may not have discovered America but we still believe some of it. Just like the bible stories are probably not true but we like them because they are good stories. It just goes to show that if we have to choose between a good story and the truth, we'll choose a good story every time.

CRITICAL RESPONSE TO TASK AND TEXT: 4

The response demonstrates a competent understanding of the main ideas in the passage and integrates those ideas with the writer's reading and experiences.

DEVELOPMENT: 4

The writer approaches development through summary, analysis, and narration and competently integrates ideas from the passage with the writer's experiences.

STRUCTURE OF RESPONSE: 4

The writer's central focus ("the author claims that history is really story telling and not the truth") competently supports the overall organization of the response. The writer's relevant ideas are grouped together and indicate a clear progression with a coherent beginning, middle, and an end.

SENTENCE AND WORD CHOICE: 4

The writer's sentences are controlled and demonstrate a little structural variety. Word choice is usually clear and conveys the writer's meaning.

GRAMMAR, USAGE, AND MECHANICS: 4

The writer demonstrates control of the rules of standard American English composition. Grammar, usage, and mechanics are usually correct. Occasional errors do not impede understanding.

In "Columbus" the author John Barrymore claims that every description of an event is from a point of view so you can never get the truth. The most you can get is a good story because every point of view are distorted. The author gives the example of Christopher Columbus who in some stories is described as a hero and in other stories is described as a villain. The version that is most valuable is the one that is most interesting.

In grade school we learn that Columbus was a great hero who discovered America and proved that the earth was round. We even celebrate Columbus Day to honor his memory. But when we get older we learn that he was giulty of some terrible crimes he killed Indians and made them into slaves. So which is the true version? We relize that we can never get the truth and that if you want to belive that Columbus was a hero then thats what you will belive because its a better story.

I think the reason why we prefer to think of Columbus as a hero instead of a villain is because we dont want to think of the man who discovered America as a killer and a slave trader even if thats what he was. History makes it up like Lincoln who was always honest or the Indians selling Manhattan for $24. We know that these things cant really be true but we perfer a good story even if its false over a true story that is boring.

The different versions of the Columbus story only proves that we can never know the truth of any historical event. But even though we can never know the truth, we can still appreciate a good story.

CRITICAL RESPONSE TO TASK AND TEXT: 3

The writer demonstrates an awareness of the main ideas in the passage, but critical engagement with those ideas is uneven and the response fails to grasp the complexity of the author's ideas. Integration of the ideas in the passage with the writer's own reading and experience is superficial and incomplete.

DEVELOPMENT: 3

The response uses some details (i.e., celebration of Columbus Day, Lincoln, and the sale of Manhattan for $24) to develop the writer's ideas, but support is generalized and uneven. The writer attempts to craft a response from the ideas in the passage, but fails to support his response with sufficient analysis or narration.

STRUCTURE OF RESPONSE: 3

The response suggests a central focus (". . . we perfer a good story even if its false over a true story that is boring"), but support is uneven and repetitive. The lack of progression of the writer's ideas indicates a basic understanding of overall essay structure.

SENTENCE AND WORD CHOICE: 3

Sentence structure lacks variety and word choice is simple though usually clear enough. The simplicity of the writer's sentences and vocabulary demonstrates a lack of understanding of the style that is possible in language.

GRAMMAR, USAGE, AND MECHANICS: 3

The response demonstrates a shaky and uneven control of language. Frequent usage errors ("its" for "it's," "cant" for "can't," "thats" for "that's"), lack of punctuation, incorrect spelling, and occasional run-ons are a little distracting.

Sample Response with Scores of 2 in All Domains

In "Columbus" the author John Barrymore explains that the description of a historical event represents a point of view. Histories give you one version of what happened but because of certain biases the description will be distorted. The truth can never be known but we can appreciate is a good story but it has nothing to do with truth.

In one version Columbus is a hero who discovers America, proves the earth is round and returns to Spain with a fortune in gold. In another version Columbus sets up slave camps and puts the slaves to work in the mines. He is responsible for the death of over 3 million natives and is arrested for brutality. In one version he discovers America and in another he doesn't.

When I was in school in D.R. we learned that Columbus was a hero who discovered the Dominican Republic and other Caribean islands. But when I came to the United States I learned that he never discover America but he still get the credit. It means to me that we get different versions but nothing is the truth. We like a good story but the truth doesnt matter. What matters is that we get a good story.

CRITICAL RESPONSE TO TASK AND TEXT: 2

The writer demonstrates a weak understanding of the ideas in the passage. The writer understands that versions of any event are variable, but the writer does not move beyond the recollection that Columbus is one thing in the D.R. and something else in the U.S. The complexity of ideas in the passage receives little treatment in the response and very little integration with the writer's own ideas and experiences.

DEVELOPMENT: 2

Approaches to development are minimal. The writer provides a brief summary that itemizes the author's main ideas, and a brief personal narrative, but development of the writer's ideas from the ideas introduced in the passage is inadequate and too general.

STRUCTURE OF RESPONSE: 2

There is an attempt to create a central focus in the third paragraph but the response does not seem organized around this central focus. The response does not demonstrate a consistent understanding of coherent essay structure.

SENTENCE AND WORD CHOICE: 2

The writer's command of sentence structure and word choice is weak. The writer's sentences show little variety and word choice is simple.

GRAMMAR, USAGE, AND MECHANICS: 2

The writer demonstrates a weak command of the rules of composition. Errors in grammar, usage, and mechanics are noticeable and distracting.

Sample Response with Scores of 1 in All Domains

The author says that the description of any event represent the points of view of the historian. It may tell the truth but you only get one version of what happen. Since any points of view is the product of specific biases like religion culture idological gender the points of view will naturally be distorted by those biases. The best we can hope for is a good story like the Christopher Columbus story.

Columbus is a hero from the school textbook. He discover America and prove the world is round and bring gold back to Spain. But he also kill Indians and make slaves and kill 3 million Indians. Columbus was arrest and is villian. Columbus is a hero and a villian.

The author say there are infinite versions of the Columbus story. But Columbus is hero and villian. The story that is valuable is the version that is most compelling meaning interesting which is that Columbus is the hero.

CRITICAL RESPONSE TO TASK AND TEXT: 1

The writer appears to understand that the passage is about infinite variations that are possible in the documentation of a historical event, but there is no integration of the ideas from the text with the writer's own ideas or experience. Most importantly, it is impossible to determine the writer's understanding of the ideas in the text since most of the response is copied from the passage. The response never gets past summary and the little summary we have is confusing.

DEVELOPMENT: 1

The writer's response to the passage introduces no ideas of his own. Therefore, it shows no approach toward development of the author's ideas through analysis or narrative.

STRUCTURE OF RESPONSE: 1

Because the writer's response lacks a central focus, or thesis, it demonstrates little organization or structure. There is no attempt to advance through a response that represents a progression or movement from beginning to end with the central focus functioning as the organizing idea.

SENTENCE AND WORD CHOICE: 1

The writer's sentences indicate little if any control. Word choice is limited. The response is mostly copied from the passage, so it is impossible to determine the writer's skill at sentence structure and word choice.

GRAMMAR, USAGE, AND MECHANICS: 1

The writer's response indicates minimal understanding of the command of language. Grammar, usage, and mechanics are mostly incorrect. The response is mostly copied from the passage so it is impossible to determine the writer's understanding of the rules of composition.

Now Try It Yourself!

In groups of two or three, select one of the essays rated 1, 2, or 3, and make suggestions for how the writer could improve the response. Remember to focus on all five areas of assessment:

- Critical response to task and text
- Development
- Structure of response
- Sentence and word choice
- Grammar, usage, and mechanics

Now Try It Yourself!

Using the suggestions your group generated, revise the response you discussed in the previous exercise.

The following passages are samples of the types of readings that you might expect to find on the CATW.

City Mouse and Country Mouse
by Max Fabian

While my wife and I were preparing for the arrival of our second child, we considered leaving the city and moving to the country. We assumed, because we had been told so many times in so many different ways, that the city and children do not mix.

A steady diet of news reports, television shows, and movies have taught us that there are significant differences between the city and the country. The city is a landscape dominated by drugs and violence, racial tension and noise. The overcrowding leads to impatience and the impatience leads to rudeness. The schools are disorderly and the parks and playgrounds are battlegrounds. Unlike the city, the country provides children with a nurturing community beyond the protective environment of the family. The neighborhood, the schools, and the civic organizations all keep children safe while educating them and ensuring for them a secure and healthy future. Who in their right mind would raise their children in a war zone when you can set down roots in a garden of paradise?

But when our second son was born, we made the decision to stay in the city. We were ready to admit that we were giving up the safety and insularity of the country, but we were more interested in the benefits of the city. We liked the energy, the opportunities for cultural exposure and awareness, and the history of the city. We believed that our kids would acquire a toughness and an alertness that would make them stronger and serve them well as they grew into adults. Most importantly, we felt that the city encouraged variation and adaptability, and if you are not exposed to the conditions that make these things possible, then you will not survive long.

WRITING DIRECTIONS

Read the passage above and write an essay responding to the ideas it presents. In your essay, be sure to summarize the passage in your own words, stating the author's most important ideas. Develop your essay by identifying one idea in the passage that you feel is especially significant, and explain its significance. Support your claims with evidence or examples drawn from what you have read, learned in school, and/or personally experienced.

Remember to review your essay and make any changes or corrections that are needed to help your reader follow your thinking. You will have 90 minutes to complete your essay.

Pink Is for Boys, Blue Is for Girls
by Claudia Caswell

Given the accepted opinion that pink is for girls, blue is for boys, it is hard to imagine things being any other way. However, some evidence suggests that these color lines actually weren't drawn until the middle of the twentieth century. In the nineteenth century, almost all babies wore white. In fact, parents back then were so unconcerned about distinguishing between the sexes that they outfitted their infant sons and daughters in dresses across the board. Even when babies started wearing colorful clothing in the mid-nineteenth century, specific colors were not identified as "male" and "female." An 1855 *New York Times* account of a "baby show" described both sexes as wearing a wide and arbitrary array of colors.

In the early twentieth century, however, male and female children's clothes began to differ stylistically—boys started wearing pants, while girls remained in dresses—and with those changes came more consistent color/gender associations. At first, though, pink was ascribed most often to boys, and blue to girls. In 1918, an article in the *Ladies' Home Journal* declared, "There has been a great diversity of opinion on the subject, but the generally accepted rule is pink for the boy and blue for the girl. The reason is that pink being a more decided and stronger color is more suitable for the boy, while blue, which is more delicate and dainty, is prettier for the girl." Another theory holds that blue, associated frequently with the Virgin Mary, was believed to reflect little girls' purity and goodness, while pink, a lighter shade of red, was seen as a better match for male children's aggressive temperament. But by the 1940s, the color alignment shifted, and society's association of pink with femininity and blue with masculinity has remained intact since then.

WRITING DIRECTIONS

Read the passage above and write an essay responding to the ideas it presents. In your essay, be sure to summarize the passage in your own words, stating the author's most important ideas. Develop your essay by identifying one idea in the passage that you feel is especially significant, and explain its significance. Support your claims with evidence or examples drawn from what you have read, learned in school, and/or personally experienced.

Remember to review your essay and make any changes or corrections that are needed to help your reader follow your thinking. You will have 90 minutes to complete your essay.

Birth Order
by Addison DeWitt

Believe it or not, there is something that influences your personality even before you take your first breath. It is your birth order. Research shows that a person's birth order has a direct link with his or her personality. Birth order is not a simple system that stereotypes all first-borns as having one personality, second-borns another, and last-born kids a third. Instead, birth order is about tendencies and general characteristics that may often apply.

First-borns may be more highly motivated to achieve than their younger siblings or may choose professions such as science, medicine, or law. A greater number of first-borns also choose careers as accountants, bookkeepers, executive secretaries, engineers, or jobs involving computers. First-borns typically go for anything that takes precision, strong powers of concentration, and exacting mental discipline. A common characteristic of a first-born is confidence in being taken seriously by those around him. It's no wonder that first-borns often go on to positions of leadership or high achievement.

The general characteristics of the middle-born child are the most varied and contradictory of all the birth positions. Characteristics may include being a mediator or one who avoids conflict, being independent *and* extremely loyal to a peer group, and frequently being the child in the family who gets "lost." This child may be shy and quiet or friendly and outgoing, impatient and easily frustrated or laid back, taking life in stride. A middle-born may be very competitive or very easygoing, the family "black sheep" or the peacemaker.

Youngest children in the family are typically the outgoing charmers, the personable manipulators. They are also affectionate, uncomplicated, and sometimes a little absent-minded. Their "space cadet" approach to life gets laughs, smiles, and shakes of the head. A typical characteristic of the last-born is that he is more carefree and vivacious—a real "people person" who is usually popular in spite of, or because of, his clowning.

Like first-borns, single children are often treated like little adults—sometimes to the point of feeling they never had a childhood. The labels describing first-borns also fit the only-born. But preceding each label—perfectionistic, reliable, conscientious, well-organized, critical, serious, scholarly, cautious, conservative—add the word *super*.

Using birth order to determine personality type is not an exact science, but it does indicate characteristics that are surprisingly accurate.

WRITING DIRECTIONS

Read the passage above and write an essay responding to the ideas it presents. In your essay, be sure to summarize the passage in your own words, stating the author's most important ideas. Develop your essay by identifying one idea in the passage that you feel is especially significant, and explain its significance. Support your claims with evidence or examples drawn from what you have read, learned in school, and/or personally experienced.

Remember to review your essay and make any changes or corrections that are needed to help your reader follow your thinking. You will have 90 minutes to complete your essay.

To Breed or Not to Breed
by Benjamin Braddock

In 1951, the population of the United States was just under 155 million people, which was double what it was in 1900. In 2011, the population passed 310 million. In other words, in just sixty years, the total number of people living in this country has doubled, and in a little over one hundred years it has quadrupled. If population growth continues at this rate, experts predict that by the year 2100, the population of the United States could reach one billion people. That's a lot of people.

The population of America is always growing. There is one birth every eight seconds and one death every twelve seconds. With this four second differential, it means that the U.S. population increases by one person every forty-five seconds. Between births, deaths, and immigration we add one new person to the population every fifteen seconds.

Some experts believe that unless certain restrictions are put in place, such as limits on family size and tighter immigration laws, the country is headed toward disaster. America's cities will be the hardest hit by overpopulation, since urban infrastructures simply cannot sustain such extreme numbers. China imposed limits on family size in 1979 and since then its general population and urban infrastructures have stabilized. In fact, India will soon pass China as the most populous nation in the world. America needs to follow China's lead.

Others take a less restrictive approach. They believe that population growth and distribution have a way of stabilizing themselves. Wars, famine, diseases, and natural disasters always occur to keep population under control. Experts agree that this is certainly not the most preemptive response to the problem because it leads to reliance upon factors beyond human control. Still, they argue that nature will provide its own solution because it always has.

Finally, there is the response that chooses to ignore the problem altogether. Since hardly anyone alive today will be here in a hundred years, no one should worry about the issue of an overpopulated America. Besides, as long as many Americans insist upon their right to have large families and as long as foreigners see America as the land of opportunity, there's nothing anyone can really do about population growth.

WRITING DIRECTIONS

Read the passage above and write an essay responding to the ideas it presents. In your essay, be sure to summarize the passage in your own words, stating the author's most important ideas. Develop your essay by identifying one idea in the passage that you feel is especially significant, and explain its significance. Support your claims with evidence or examples drawn from what you have read, learned in school, and/or personally experienced.

Remember to review your essay and make any changes or corrections that are needed to help your reader follow your thinking. You will have 90 minutes to complete your essay.

Working Class Hero
by Donny Kerabatsos

Steven Slater looks nothing like what we imagine a spokesman for the working class should look like. What he does look like is exactly what he is, or was that is, until August 9, 2010—a flight attendant. But when Steven Slater cursed out an unruly passenger over the plane's loudspeakers, grabbed two beers, and slid down the plane's emergency exit, he performed what many recognized as an act of working class heroism. He was later arrested and formally fired, but for the next three days he was the lead story on the evening news and his face appeared on the cover of every newspaper in America.

Slater's gestures were reckless and probably a little nutty. In our current difficult economic times, quitting your job without a new one to step into usually leads to a long period of unemployment. Doing it the way Slater did it only compounds the problem. But still, Slater's tantrum inspired tremendous curiosity and support. Within a week, 30,000 people had joined the Free Steven Slater site on Facebook.

Slater did what so many stressed out, overworked, underpaid American workers wish they could do but can't. He shouted back. Those who still have jobs work harder and longer than ever before while wages remain the same. Massive layoffs and hiring freezes have taught them to smile and keep their mouths shut. If they protest, they might expect to join the millions of others who are looking for work. Steven Slater has himself joined the ranks of those unemployed, but he did so with a flourish. Some may think he was reckless and even foolish; those who understand Steven Slater's frustration recognize him as a type of working class hero.

WRITING DIRECTIONS

Read the passage above and write an essay responding to the ideas it presents. In your essay, be sure to summarize the passage in your own words, stating the author's most important ideas. Develop your essay by identifying one idea in the passage that you feel is especially significant, and explain its significance. Support your claims with evidence or examples drawn from what you have read, learned in school, and/or personally experienced.

Remember to review your essay and make any changes or corrections that are needed to help your reader follow your thinking. You will have 90 minutes to complete your essay.

Superheroes
by Lloyd Richards

All you need to do is attend a child's costume party to realize that children enjoy a special relationship with superheroes. For children, the attraction of the superhero, I believe, lies in his show of strength and fearlessness. The child admires in the superhero the qualities that the child knows it lacks. Trembling before the terrors of the world around him, the misfit child recognizes his own weakness. The mask and the costume grant special powers, protecting him like a suit of armor. The moment he takes off the mask, however, the illusion is shattered by the screaming mother or the angry father, the cranky teacher or the schoolyard bully. But the child has taken something away from this exchange of identities. His identification with the superhero has taught him that he is weak, that others are strong, but that one day he will be strong and that he will be able to make decisions for himself. He only needs to be patient. His time will come.

The superhero also presents fascinations for the adult, but it is very different from the attraction it holds for the child. The adult knows that his time has not yet come. In fact, he suspects that it might never come. The things he wanted he realizes he cannot have and the things that he likes he is unable to share with anyone. He understands that these desires and secrets threaten to set him apart from everyone else. This makes him uneasy, even ashamed. He is different, just as Batman and Superman and Spiderman are all different in the demonstration of their unique super powers. But like Batman and Superman and Spiderman, the adult must conceal this difference. If his private life were ever revealed, he would lose his membership in the most important community of all—the human community. Just as the child attempts to conceal his weakness behind a mask, the adult attempts to hide his differences behind his public identity, the same identity that he exposes as he takes the train to work, carries out his meaningless job, and eats dinner with his ungrateful family. So the adult wears a mask, the Bruce Wayne, Clark Kent, Peter Parker mask, and hopes that no one ever discovers his secret life, in which he daydreams about what is forbidden and prefers the things that he cannot reveal.

WRITING DIRECTIONS

Read the passage above and write an essay responding to the ideas it presents. In your essay, be sure to summarize the passage in your own words, stating the author's most important ideas. Develop your essay by identifying one idea in the passage that you feel is especially significant, and explain its significance. Support your claims with evidence or examples drawn from what you have read, learned in school, and/or personally experienced.

Remember to review your essay and make any changes or corrections that are needed to help your reader follow your thinking. You will have 90 minutes to complete your essay.

Little Things Matter
by Guy Haines

In his essay "Why Do Men Stupefy Themselves?" the great Russian writer Leo Tolstoy speaks of the importance of small events in determining significant outcomes. History books and public and private memory usually give credit to the major events. But the little things that we rarely ever notice, the tiny things that almost slip by, are just as noteworthy, both historically and personally.

Tolstoy writes of the artist Bryullóv who corrected a student's drawing by making the smallest change. The student exclaimed: "Why, you only touched it a little bit, but it is a completely different thing." Bryullóv replied: "Art begins where the tiny bit begins."

Tolstoy claims that the same observation of art applies to life. True life begins with the barely noticeable—the things that matter are the things we barely see. Life is not lived as a series of great moments—where people fight and slay one another—it is lived in between the great occurrences where small changes take place.

Another way of thinking about this passage by Tolstoy is to imagine the course of our own lives. We are born, we graduate from school, we land our first important job, we marry, we have children, we retire, we die. These are the major events. But are these the really important moments of our lives? Are not the things we take pleasure in remembering, the things that we think of as contributing to what we think of as our identity and our lives, the stuff lived in between these major events? It is rather the small things that matter, that make us smile and cry, and that give our lives meaning. The big things are just there to frame them.

WRITING DIRECTIONS

Read the passage above and write an essay responding to the ideas it presents. In your essay, be sure to summarize the passage in your own words, stating the author's most important ideas. Develop your essay by identifying one idea in the passage that you feel is especially significant, and explain its significance. Support your claims with evidence or examples drawn from what you have read, learned in school, and/or personally experienced.

Remember to review your essay and make any changes or corrections that are needed to help your reader follow your thinking. You will have 90 minutes to complete your essay.

The New Face of Fame
by Mel Cooley

When the American artist Andy Warhol predicted that "in the future, everyone will be world-famous for fifteen minutes," he could not have imagined that reality TV, whatever that is, would make this possible. The twenty-first-century celebrity is the product, or victim, of this new form of entertainment. We recognize it by its most obvious feature: bad taste.

Kim Kardashian gained her first fifteen minutes of fame by circulating pornographic videos of herself. Since then, she has stayed current by always being photographed in the most flattering light and saying as little as necessary in order to avoid giving the impression that she has nothing to say. As long as she continues smiling and keeping her regular appointments with her personal trainer, her hair stylist, and her plastic surgeon, she will probably continue to arouse us with her talentless presence.

Reality TV has introduced a new type of celebrity: the public laughingstock. We have a fascinating example of this in the form of the diminutive Snooki, though what exactly it is that Snooki does that makes her so fascinating is still not clear. Her co-stars on the reality show *Jersey Shore* do not exactly set her apart by offering counterexamples of elegance and grace, brains and beauty. Perhaps Snooki is as popular as she is because she reminds us that public embarrassment is a perfectly valid form of prime-time entertainment.

Finally, there is the group of celebrities who make up the population known as the Real Housewives. My mother was a housewife and she was real, but she did not look or behave like the women on these television shows. My mother was too busy doing the things that really real housewives do, like clean and cook and raise a family. She had no time to worry about applying additional layers of makeup, changing her costume jewelry every half hour, and spreading vicious rumors about her neighbors. Perhaps what the Real Housewives of New York and Miami and Orange County teach us is that it is possible to be real and a housewife without being either.

As long as you are not willing to let a lack of intelligence, talent, or grace get in the way, then fifteen minutes of fame is available. All you need to do is conquer your shame.

WRITING DIRECTIONS

Read the passage above and write an essay responding to the ideas it presents. In your essay, be sure to summarize the passage in your own words, stating the author's most important ideas. Develop your essay by identifying one idea in the passage that you feel is especially significant, and explain its significance. Support your claims with evidence or examples drawn from what you have read, learned in school, and/or personally experienced.

Remember to review your essay and make any changes or corrections that are needed to help your reader follow your thinking. You will have 90 minutes to complete your essay.

I Am Not a Role Model
by Walter Sobchak

Back in the early nineties, when Charles Barkley was playing professional basketball, he dared to question the responsibility of athletes to serve as role models for kids. Barkley challenged the assumption that professional athletes should behave and think of themselves in a certain way that encourages a kid to look up to them as models of correct behavior. "A million guys can dunk a basketball in jail; should they be role models?" he asked. He urged parents and teachers to step up and be role models themselves to their own kids. "What they (parents and the media) are really doing is telling kids to look up to someone they can't become, because not many people can be like we are. Kids can't be like Michael Jordan."

Harry von Zell, noted child psychologist, agrees with Barkley. Apart from the fact that all athletes, like all of us, are very flawed individuals, there is the reality that the identity of the athlete is just a small component of the entire person. The athlete is an invention of the fans, the media, and the athletes themselves. They don't really exist outside of our own hero worshipping imaginations. "There is this misconception," claims von Zell, "that just because an athlete can run fast, hit a ball far, or dunk a basketball, that he or she is a great person and should be imitated. We are surprised and disappointed when the star athlete is exposed as an alcoholic, a gambler, or just someone who made a bad decision." Von Zell concedes that it is the job of the athlete to be an athlete, not to be a father or mother figure and especially not a saint.

But George Fenneman, sports psychologist, disagrees. He admits that all that von Zell says is true, but there is still the reality of the child's imagination which needs to believe that his or her favorite athletes are god, with god-like abilities. Even if athletes know that their abilities do not define them as a complete human being, they must know that children admire whatever they do. This confers upon athletes the unique responsibility of living up to an ideal, even if it is false. "As long as athletes are not asked to heal a crippled child with their magic touch or do not promise to hit three home runs for a kid in the hospital, then are we asking too much of these million dollar babies to behave with a sense of grace and dignity? Besides," adds Fenneman, "if athletes can behave with these ideals in mind, isn't it possible that they might become better people, after all? Won't this make them suitable role models anyway?"

WRITING DIRECTIONS

Read the passage above and write an essay responding to the ideas it presents. In your essay, be sure to summarize the passage in your own words, stating the author's most important ideas. Develop your essay by identifying one idea in the passage that you feel is especially significant, and explain its significance. Support your claims with evidence or examples drawn from what you have read, learned in school, and/or personally experienced.

Remember to review your essay and make any changes or corrections that are needed to help your reader follow your thinking. You will have 90 minutes to complete your essay.

The Imp of the Perverse
by Theodore Bundy

In his short story "The Imp of the Perverse," Edgar Allan Poe describes the desire of people to do exactly the wrong thing, knowing that it is the wrong thing, in any given situation. The impulse is compared to an *imp*, or devil, which leads an otherwise decent person into mischief. We know that what we are contemplating is wrong. We know that if we do the thing we are not supposed to do, we will be caught. We know that when we are caught it will mean the end of all our freedoms. We will be punished. We do it anyway. We can't help it. It is "the imp of the perverse."

Some would argue that "the imp of the perverse" is a convenient way of assigning blame to something, namely the imp, which allows the guilty person to escape self-reproach. "If I am not responsible for this wrong act, if it was the result of some agency that moved me, against my will, to the performance of the crime, well then, how can I be held responsible?" Certainly the villain did this thing, he knew it was wrong, but he was driven, he would say, by the devil. "It's not my fault," he would say. "I am innocent. The imp, or devil, made me do it."

On the other hand, "the imp of the perverse" is just a metaphor that is a perfectly valid psychological explanation for any illegal act. Since every human being is the product of influences that work on his or her personality from the outside, the behavior of human beings can be determined by studying those influences. If we say that a bad home life or an unhappy marriage or an inattentive school system participated in the creation of a damaged personality, aren't we using the argument of "the imp of the perverse"? We are arguing, essentially, that everyone knows right from wrong. But we are also saying that forces beyond the control of the individual led to the commission of his crime. He was not responsible. It was that dreaded imp.

Poe was playing games with us when he wrote "The Imp of the Perverse." He knew that people will lie to themselves and create excuses in order to justify their actions. That is why they create imps. But we have also enabled an entire system of justification. We create our own imps when we try to escape responsibility for our actions by assigning the blame to our psychological demons.

WRITING DIRECTIONS

Read the passage above and write an essay responding to the ideas it presents. In your essay, be sure to summarize the passage in your own words, stating the author's most important ideas. Develop your essay by identifying one idea in the passage that you feel is especially significant, and explain its significance. Support your claims with evidence or examples drawn from what you have read, learned in school, and/or personally experienced.

Remember to review your essay and make any changes or corrections that are needed to help your reader follow your thinking. You will have 90 minutes to complete your essay.

8 Correcting Common Errors

This section reviews some errors that are frequently found in essay responses. At the end of each section, you will find links to exercises that will help you work on these common errors. The exercises are from Bedford/St. Martin's Web site *Re:Writing*, a resource for writing students. You will need to register with the site in order to use its resources, but registration is free and easy. Go to the *Exercise Central* home page at **bedfordstmartins.com/exercisecentral/** to get started.

Sentence Fragments

A sentence must include at least one independent clause: It must have a subject and a verb, and it must also be able to stand alone as a complete thought.

```
subj.  verb
 ┌┴┐  ┌─┴─┐
```
➤ He ordered a bowl of soup.

This is an independent clause. It has a subject, *he*, and a verb, *ordered*, and it does not need any more information to complete the thought.

A sentence fragment occurs when either the subject or verb (or both) is missing, or when a subordinating word or phrase makes the word string incomplete.

Has a subject but no verb

➤ The bowl of soup.

Has a verb but no subject

➤ Landed in his lap.

Begins with a subordinating word

➤ After he ordered the bowl of soup.

Consider the following sentence:

```
subord. conj.
 ┌───┴──┐
```
➤ After he ordered a bowl of soup.

This sentence is a fragment: Although it has a subject and a verb (*he* and *ordered*), it is incomplete because it begins with a subordinating conjunction, *after*. Someone who reads this sentence might respond, "After he ordered a bowl of soup *WHAT?*"

You can fix this fragment by deleting the subordinating word or phrase, adding what is missing, or connecting it to another independent clause.

➤ ~~After he~~ *He* ordered a bowl of soup.

➤ After he ordered a bowl of soup/ *, he ordered a burger.*

➤ After he ordered a bowl of soup/ *, he* ~~He~~ *ordered a burger.*

ind. clause

As you edit and proofread your essay exam (and everything else you write), check to make sure that you have corrected any sentence fragments. To practice correcting sentence fragments, go to *Exercise Central*, click on a study plan, and type *fragment* in the search box.

bedfordstmartins.com/exercisecentral/

Run-On Sentences

A run-on sentence is one or more independent clauses that have not been joined correctly. There are two types of run-on sentences: **fused sentences** and **comma splices**. A fused sentence occurs when two independent clauses are joined without any punctuation at all:

➤ The film festival begins on Sunday evening it will end the following Saturday afternoon.

A comma splice occurs when two independent clauses are linked by a comma:

➤ The film festival begins on Sunday evening, it will end the following Saturday afternoon.

To fix run-on sentences, you can do one of four things:

1. You can insert a period at the end of the first independent clause:

➤ The film festival begins on Sunday evening. It will end the following Saturday afternoon.

2. You can insert a semicolon between the two independent clauses:

➤ The film festival begins on Sunday evening; it will end the following Saturday afternoon.

3. You can insert a comma and a coordinating conjunction (*for, and, nor, but, or, yet*) at the end of the first independent clause:

   ➤ The film festival begins on Sunday evening, <u>and</u> it will end the following Saturday afternoon.

4. You can add a subordinating conjunction to the beginning of the sentence:

   ➤ <u>Even though</u> the film festival begins on Sunday evening, it will end the following Saturday afternoon.

As you edit and proofread your essay exam (and everything else you write), check to make sure that you have corrected any run-on sentences. To practice correcting run-on sentences, go to *Exercise Central*, click on a study plan, and type *run-on* in the search box.

bedfordstmartins.com/exercisecentral/

Subject-Verb Agreement

It is not enough for a sentence to have a subject and a verb; the subject and verb must agree. That is, if the subject is singular (*I, you, he/she/it*), the verb must be in the singular form, and if the subject is plural (*we, you, they*), the verb must be in the plural form.

```
             subj.   verb
              |       |
➤  SINGULAR  The pilot prepares for takeoff.
```

```
             subj.   verb
              |       |
➤  PLURAL   The pilots prepare for takeoff.
```

The subject in the first sentence, *pilot*, is singular, so the verb, *prepares*, must be singular, too. The subject in the second sentence, *pilots*, is plural, so the verb, *prepare*, must be plural, too.

Native speakers of English will generally recognize when a subject and verb agree, but occasionally the structure of the sentence can be confusing.

Subjects joined with *and* are generally plural:

   are
➤ Fred and Wilma ~~is~~ lovely together.
                   ^

Collective nouns (such as *family* or *couple*) are singular:

   is
➤ The couple ~~are~~ traveling to Hawaii immediately after the party.
              ^

Most indefinite pronouns (such as *anybody, each, no one, someone*) are singular, so they take a singular verb:

>   *is*
> ➤   Each of the bridesmaids ~~are~~ pretty.

Notice that when a word or phrase comes between the subject and the verb, as in the example above, the form the verb should take isn't immediately clear. Should it be plural to match *bridesmaids* or singular to match *each*? Even though *bridesmaids* is closer to the verb, *each* is the subject of the sentence, so the verb should be singular, not plural.

    The relative pronouns *who, which,* and *that* often create problems with subject-verb agreement. When a relative pronoun is the subject of a subordinate clause, the verb in that clause should agree with the noun or pronoun that the relative pronoun is replacing:

>   antecedent
>   *fulfill*
> ➤   You should register for classes that ~~fulfills~~ the requirements of your major.

The verb *fulfill* should agree with *classes.*

    As you edit and proofread your essay exam (and everything else you write), check to make sure that you have corrected any subject-verb agreement errors. To practice correcting errors of subject-verb agreement, go to *Exercise Central*, click on a study plan, and type *subject-verb agreement* in the search box.

bedfordstmartins.com/exercisecentral/

Possessives

Possessive nouns indicate ownership or possession. The easiest way to determine whether a noun should be possessive is to test it by turning it into an *of* phrase:

The <u>dog's owner</u> entered the park.   The <u>owner of the dog</u> entered the park.

Both sentences describe the same relationship between the dog and its owner, so the word *dog* should be possessive: *dog's.*

To make a singular noun possessive, add *-'s,* whether the word ends in *-s* or not.

> ➤   the *teacher's* apartment
> ➤   the *boss's* wife

To make a plural noun possessive, add an apostrophe at the end of the word:

> ➤ the *teachers'* lounge
> ➤ the *bosses'* wives

Most native English speakers know when a noun should be possessive, but occasionally determining which noun should be possessive is tricky.

When the subject is compound (*Fred and Wilma*) and ownership is joint, make the last noun in the sequence possessive:

> ➤ Fred and Wilma's wedding was lovely.

When the subject is compound and ownership is individual, make both nouns possessive:

> ➤ Fred's and Wilma's pets are noisy.

As you edit and proofread your essay exam (and everything else you write), check to make sure that you have corrected any errors with possession. To practice correcting errors of possession, go to *Exercise Central*, click on a study plan, and type *possession* in the search box.

bedfordstmartins.com/exercisecentral/

Pronoun-Antecedent Agreement

When a pronoun replaces the noun that precedes it, the pronoun must agree in number and gender with that noun. (The noun in cases like this is called the **antecedent** because it is the noun that *comes before* the pronoun). Generally, matching pronouns to their antecedents is straightforward. Most English speakers wouldn't have trouble with sentences like these:

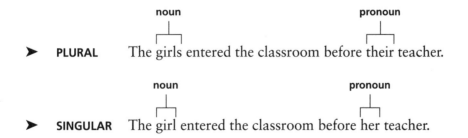

> ➤ **PLURAL**   The girls entered the classroom before their teacher.

> ➤ **SINGULAR**   The girl entered the classroom before her teacher.

In the first sentence, the plural pronoun *their* replaces the plural noun *girls*. In the second sentence, the singular, feminine pronoun *her* replaces the singular, feminine noun *girl*.

Errors usually occur when pronouns replace **indefinite pronouns** (like *anybody, each, neither, nothing,* and *someone*) that do not refer to specific people or things or **generic nouns** (like *astronaut, executive, nurse,* and *student*) that refer to a typical member of a group. Indefinite pronouns are singular, so the pronouns that replace them must also be singular. They are also gender neutral, so masculine pronouns won't work either. To avoid agreement problems, use *he or she* or *his or her*, or rewrite the sentence to avoid the indefinite pronoun:

                                                       his or her

➤   *Anyone* who goes to Alaska in February should have ~~their~~ head examined.

Notice that the indefinite pronoun also takes the singular verb form, *goes*.

        All professors expect

➤   ~~*Everybody* expects~~ *their* students to study for the final exam.

As you edit and proofread your essay exam (and everything else you write), check to make sure that you have corrected any errors of pronoun-antecedent agreement. To practice correcting errors of pronoun-antecedent agreement, go to *Exercise Central*, click on a study plan, and type *pronoun-antecedent* in the search box.

bedfordstmartins.com/exercisecentral/

Some Commonly Confused Words

As you proofread your essay, watch out for these commonly confused words:

accept, except	*Accept* means "to receive;" *except* means "excluding."
affect, effect	*Affect* generally means "to influence;" *effect* can be a verb meaning "to bring about" or a noun meaning "result."
all ready, already	*All ready* means "prepared;" *already* means "previously."
all together, altogether	*All together* means "all in one place;" *altogether* means "entirely."
allusion, illusion	*Allusion* means "indirect reference;" *illusion* means "false impression" or "false appearance."
amoral, immoral	*Amoral* means "neither moral nor immoral;" *immoral* means "not moral."
amount, number	*Amount* is used with noncount nouns (for example, *What amount of beer did they drink?*); *number* is used with count nouns (for example, *They drank a large number of beers.*).
among, between	*Among* is used with three or more options; *between* is used with two options.
cite, site	*Cite* means "to quote an example or authority;" *site* means "location" (often short for "Web site").
climactic, climatic	*Climactic* refers to a climax; *climatic* refers to climate.
coarse, course	*Coarse* means "rough;" *course* means "path, route."
explicit, implicit	*Explicit* means "stated directly;" *implicit* means "implied."
fewer, less	*Fewer* is used with count nouns (for example, *He wishes he drank fewer beers.*); *less* is used with noncount nouns (for example, *He wishes he drank less beer.*).
good, well	*Good* is an adjective (*the good wife*); *well* is an adverb (*She did well on her exam.*).
imply, infer	*Imply* means "to state indirectly;" *infer* means "to derive a conclusion."
its, it's	*Its* is the possessive form of the word *it*; *it's* is a contraction of *it is*.
lay, lie	*Lay* means "to place;" *lie* can be either a noun meaning "a falsehood" or a verb meaning "to recline."
loose, lose	*Loose* means "not tight;" *lose* means "to mislay" or "to misplace," or the opposite of "to win."
passed, past	*Passed* is the past tense of the verb "to pass;" *past* is either a noun meaning "a time gone by" or a preposition meaning "beyond" (*The school is just past the library.*).

precede, proceed	*Precede* means "to go before;" *proceed* means "to continue" or "to advance."
principal, principle	*Principal* as an adjective means "chief" or "most important"; *principal* as a noun means "chief" or "head," usually of a school; *principle*, a noun, means "rule" or "law."
sensual, sensuous	*Sensual* means "indulging the senses;" *sensuous* means "gratifying the senses" in terms of artistic pleasure.
their, they're, there	*Their* is a possessive pronoun (for example, *their dog*); *they're* is a contraction of *they are*; and *there* is an adverb of place meaning "in that location."
then, than	*Then* is an adverb meaning "at that time" or "soon after" (for example, *First we got married and then we fell in love.*); *than* is a comparative conjunction (for example, *I am taller than my sister.*).
to, too, two	*To* is a preposition; *too* is an adverb meaning "besides" or "excessively;" and *two* is a number between one and three.
who's, whose	*Who's* is a contraction of *who is*; *whose* is a possessive pronoun (for example, *Whose shoe is that?*).
your, you're	*Your* is a possessive pronoun (for example, *Your order is ready.*); *you're* is a contraction of *you are*.

Some Commonly Misspelled Words

As you proofread your essay, look for these commonly misspelled words and correct them if necessary:

absence	eligible	mischievous	referred
accommodate	embarrass	necessary	restaurant
achievement	exaggerate	noticeable	rhythm
acknowledge	exercise	occasion	sandwich
acquire	exhaust	occurred	seize
all right	extraordinary	occurrence	separate
analyze	fascinate	parallel	sergeant
apparently	February	particularly	siege
arctic	foreign	pastime	sincerely
ascend	forty	permanent	strictly
beautiful	fourth	permissible	subtly
believe	grammar	perseverance	succeed
benefited	guard	phenomenon	thorough
bureau	guarantee	playwright	tragedy
business	harass	precede	transferred
cemetery	height	preference	tries
commitment	indispensable	preferred	truly
committed	inevitable	presence	unnecessarily
committee	irrelevant	prevalent	usually
conceivable	irresistible	privilege	vacuum
criticize	knowledge	proceed	villain
definitely	library	pronunciation	weird
descendant	license	quiet	whether
desperate	lightning	quite	
disastrous	maintenance	receive	
eighth	maneuver	recognize	

Answers to Some of the Exercises in Chapter 5

Corrected Paragraph from Page 36

The lottery is, in fact, designed for people to lose. After all, its primary function is to raise revenue for government operations, not to make people rich. It is not impossible to win, but the odds against winning are astronomical: At worst, it's 1 chance in 175 million! Players have a better chance of being hit by lightning.

Corrected Paragraph from Page 36

I realize that many students at New York Community College hardly seem to want an education. They are here because it is better than the other options. Maybe their parents wanted them to go to college just to get them out of the house. Maybe their friends are at the school and they just want to hang out. Maybe it is just their way of putting off having to go to work full-time. Most of these students actually go to their classes, but many are not involved and just sit in the back of the classroom and text message on their phones. They just come and put in an appearance though they don't have any commitment to their work. These kinds of students don't do much for the college and do less for themselves.

   I suppose there must be other reasons why students are at New York Community College, but for most students it has more to do with the diploma than the learning. I am here partly for the diploma but mostly for the education. I know what I need to do because I have been told by my teachers and parents that you cannot get anywhere in life if you don't get an education. I have wasted enough time already. I am going to try very hard to get everything I can out of college. I may never have another chance to go to school full-time again. I am going to make the most of this opportunity.

Corrected Paragraph from Page 37

There are at least three good reasons why young children should not watch more than an hour of television per day. First, placing a limitation on children's television habits will enable them to explore other activities that they would not even know about if they spent too much time staring at the television. For instance, a child could spend more time outside exploring nature and get exercise at the same time. Children can also read books and learn from them what they could never learn from television. Second, watching television is an isolating experience, even when there are other children present. A child could have more friends and get to know them better if he or she were able to interact with them instead of everyone staring at the television screen. Finally, children will enjoy the shows they do watch and they will learn to be more selective in their choice of programs. This is especially important since they will almost certainly be lifelong television viewers. They can either benefit or suffer from their viewing habits. After all, we don't want children to eat only junk food, so why allow them to digest unlimited amounts of television junk?